Eye on the Sky

*How
Aircraft
Controllers
Work*

EYE ON THE SKY

How Aircraft Controllers Work

Creighton Peet

Macrae Smith Company • Philadelphia

The author wishes to thank the following people for their technical assistance in preparing this book: Controllers John F. Leyden and James Knoetgen; Federal Aviation Administration specialists Howard G. Eisbrouch, Walter Buechler, Robert Fulton, Frank Puglisi, and H. E. Henneman of the Denver, Colorado, Center. Also, Captain William Sonneman of TWA and Mr. Ivan W. Fickett of BOAC. And finally, Miss Joanne Gravino, the FAA secretary who knows everything.

Copyright © 1970 by Creighton Peet

Library of Congress Catalog Card Number 70-108863
Manufactured in the United States of America
Trade SBN: 8255-7200-2
Library Edition SBN: 8255-7201-0

Book design by William E. Lickfield

Contents

Eye on the Sky

Hunched over the black disc of his radarscope, with only its faint greenish glow lighting his face, an aircraft controller sits in a dimly lit, windowless room, endlessly unraveling a fantastic three-dimensional traffic jam. Before him five, ten or even fifteen pairs of little blips of bright light—"slashes" —are crawling slowly across his scope.

Each pair of blips represents a plane in flight. Some of these planes may be a hundred miles away, thousands of feet in the air, and flying at almost the speed of sound. Others may be only five or ten miles away and losing speed rapidly as they slide down an invisible "glide path" to land on a nearby runway.

The radar approach controller never sees any of these planes, and most of the passengers whose lives are in his hands do not even know he exists. Only the pilots, who have been talking with him and other controllers continuously by radio, understand how important he has been in bringing their planes down safely.

Despite roomfuls of electronic equipment on the ground and the incredibly intelligent devices on the plane, the almost 9,000 radar controllers and their 11,000 assistants, flight data aids and supervisors watching radarscopes in darkened rooms all over the United States are still absolutely essential.

Computers remember hundreds of essential facts and perform complicated calculations instantly. Pilots are highly skilled and know exactly what their planes can do. But every few minutes when a big transport is making an approach for a landing, its captain must depend on the instantaneous decisions of a controller who is following on his scope not only the pilot's own plane but a dozen other planes flying through the nearby airspace. And all of these planes must be provided with a safe "separation" or distance from any other plane.

This means that every pilot must be kept at least three

Corner of the New York Center's big aircraft control radar room at Ronkonkomo, L.I., about 10:30 in the evening when pressure on controllers has let up

CREIGHTON PEET

to five miles behind the plane ahead of him and a thousand feet above or below any other plane near him. Out in the open country or over the ocean this is a different problem. But snaking your way into a lineup of planes dropping down from 25,000 feet and moving at five hundred to six hundred miles an hour to ground level and a dead stop—this is when a pilot really needs help. With planes approaching an airport from every direction it is a hair-raising job. And if he stops to think, a controller remembers that nearly half of all fatal airline crashes occur during a landing.

Controllers must be intelligent and so well-trained that they do the right thing instinctively. And they must be aggressive and follow through. A few seconds of fluttering indecision could bring disaster to a jetliner groping its way through the smog above a big city airport. The controller must come up instantly with instructions—the right instruc-

A radar control room may have a dozen or as many as fifty men working in the darkness.
LOS ANGELES DEPT. OF AIRPORTS

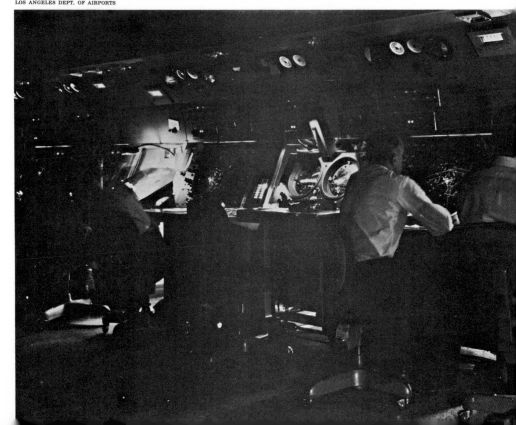

tions. He tells pilots when to turn right or left, when to cut their speed, and when to descend to a lower altitude. That is, he "talks a plane down" to a safe landing on a runway—most of the time.

But if the landing approaches to an airport are already crowded with incoming planes, he may stop a plane before it gets too close to the airport and send it off to circle in a holding pattern, usually many miles away, until there is space for it to land. We will find out more about this later.

But this is only part of a controller's work. Every few minutes he gets a "handoff" of a new plane from a controller in another Sector. He gets this first from his coordinator, also known as his "H" or handoff man, who is sitting with him. The handoff man (also a radar controller), has had a phone call from a nearby Sector from which this new plane is on its way. That Sector's controller has reported that this particular plane was near such-and-such a point on the scope. So the coordinator finds what he thinks is this new plane on the scope and points it out to the controller. At the same time he hands him a paper strip about eight inches long clipped into a little plastic holder. This Strip, known as a Flight Progress Strip, is one of about half a dozen identical Strips printed much earlier in the day by the computer. They show the airline's initials, the plane's flight number, its destination, and other facts. For the last hour or so this Flight Strip and those of many other planes have been stored in a rack over this controller's radarscope. The coordinator pulled out the strip representing the plane he had heard about over the phone.

However, the controller isn't positive which of the blips on his scope checks with the new plane and the Flight Strip, and he has to be absolutely sure. So, reading, for instance, "UA256" on the Flight Strip, he talks into his telephone headset (which he wears all day), and says, "United Airlines 256—SQUAWK IDENT!" This means "United Airlines flight 256, please identify yourself."

When the pilot of flight 256 hears this message in his earphones, he pushes a little red button on the control panel just above his head. The button operates a device called a *transponder.* For a few seconds the transponder broadcasts a special signal from this plane.

The signal shows up on the controller's radarscope, making the plane's blips change from looking like this $=$ to this ■ . Now this plane stands out from all the others on his scope. For a few seconds it's a small, bright rectangle of light. The controller is now positive it represents United Airlines flight 256 and, depending on his equipment, he checks to make sure it is properly identified from now on. If his radar room uses the manual method, he covers the bright rectangle with a small transparent plastic marker called a "shrimp boat," on which, with a wax pencil, he writes important facts about this flight. The data might include the airline's initials and the number of the flight. As the blips move across his scope, he pushes the shrimp boats along to keep up with them.

Long practice enables a controller to understand instantly markings on his scope that would be meaningless to the ordinary person.

LOS ANGELES DEPT. OF AIRPORTS

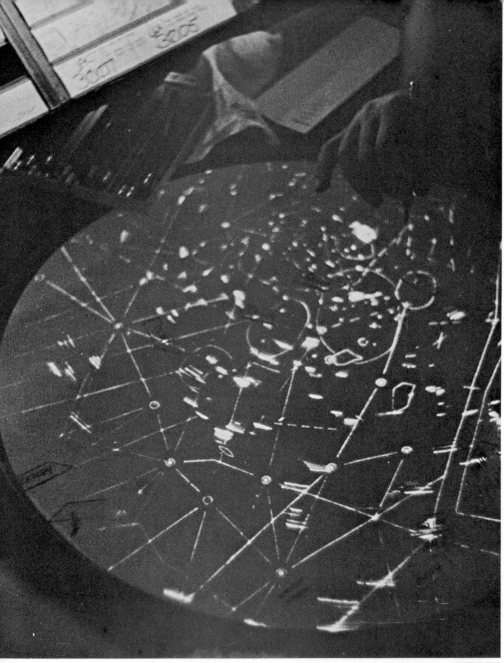

Controller placing a shrimp boat on his scope. Since these markers are clear plastic, they are hard for an outsider to see, but a couple show up clearly at the lower left.

However, if the radar room he is in is equipped with the alphanumerics system, he will find all the identifying data he needs right on the face of his scope in glowing letters of light. The most important information of all will be the plane's altitude, appearing in constantly changing numbers as it flies higher or lower. We will find out more about alphanumerics later.

While new planes are constantly appearing on his scope, others are disappearing, either because they are passing into another controller's airspace or because they have landed. In either case the controller removes such planes' Flight Strips from the active traffic storage rack when he is no longer a factor in their control. At this point he will take the Strips in their holders and toss them into a special wastebasket.

But this is not the end of these Strips, by any means. Every little while a man comes by and empties all these special wastebaskets into a box, and later all the Strips are filed away as important records of that day's flights.

However, as long as a plane is in the air it is represented by a Strip held by one controller or another—maybe in California or Missouri or Georgia or Vermont. If the plane has moved into a nearby Sector, another of the half dozen Strips first printed will be used by the next controller to handle it. But if it is passing to a distant controller, perhaps hundreds of miles away, the computer will contact the computer in that distant radar room, which will print a whole new set of Strips for this particular plane. As a plane flies between Los Angeles and New York it may be in the care of twenty to twenty-five different controllers during the five to six hours the flight takes.

Flight Progress Strips and tapes of all controller-pilot conversations are saved for at least two weeks, and some other records of controller operations are saved for about three years. Such records fill up a good part of a fair-sized room in each big airport. Of course if there is an accident, or a report of a "near miss," all tapes involved are called for by the investigator.

How Air Traffic Is Regulated

Looking up at a single plane sliding through the sky, it seems that there must be plenty of empty air space for everybody. But realizing that there are over 120,000 private and commercial planes in the United States, with more being added every day, many of which are flying between 400 and 600 miles an hour, one understands that there is not as much sky as one thought. At these speeds you run out of airspace in a hurry, and around airports the congestion is often terrific.

The need for a reliable system of air control really began to concern people seriously in the 1930s, major centers being in Newark, Chicago and Cleveland. The first primitive control towers were operated by cities, counties, or states. Traffic at an airport was "controlled" by men waving flags on a runway, lights, sirens, and even steam whistles. All contact with pilots was through the airline dispatchers, and controllers had neither radio to talk to pilots nor radar to watch planes in the air. Movements of aircraft in and out of New York City ran to only fifty to sixty operations a day. Edward A. Westlake, an old-time pilot who later spent most of his life with the Federal Aviation Administration Air Traffic Service, recalls that a flight he made from Oakland, California, to New York in 1930 took twenty-eight hours and involved thirteen stops with no gourmet meals—only a box lunch and a thermos of coffee.

At the time the Federal Government took charge of air traffic control, on July 6, 1936, controllers kept track of arriving and departing flights with blackboard notes and by moving little blocks of wood representing planes across maps spread out on tables. About that time a limited teletype system between a few Eastern cities also was set up. Federal operation came at the request of the airlines themselves, who realized that their system of monitoring only their own planes was of no use as aircraft began to multiply.

What started out as the Bureau of Air Commerce is now the Federal Aviation Administration (FAA), under the Department of Transportation. Today this agency makes the flight rules for all aircraft, both private and commercial, and operates and pays for all aircraft control facilities in both Centers and airports. The FAA even controls the flight of military planes in the United States, including *Air Force One,* used by the President, and the plane used by the Vice President. Controllers watch these planes with special care and keep all other aircraft at a greater distance than usual when they are in flight.

First of all, there are two kinds of air traffic radar control rooms. To regulate traffic in the vast, trackless ocean of airspace over the continental United States, the sky has been divided into 21 Centers—plus two more over Alaska, and one each over Hawaii, Guam, Puerto Rico and Balboa (Canal Zone), which makes a total of 27 Centers. Each Center is an irregularly shaped chunk of airspace that may cover parts of several states.

The Centers are called simply the New York Center, the

Antennas above the New York Center's radar room pick up signals relayed from other antennas hundreds of miles away.

Revolving radar antenna supplying signals to the radar room at the Indianapolis Center

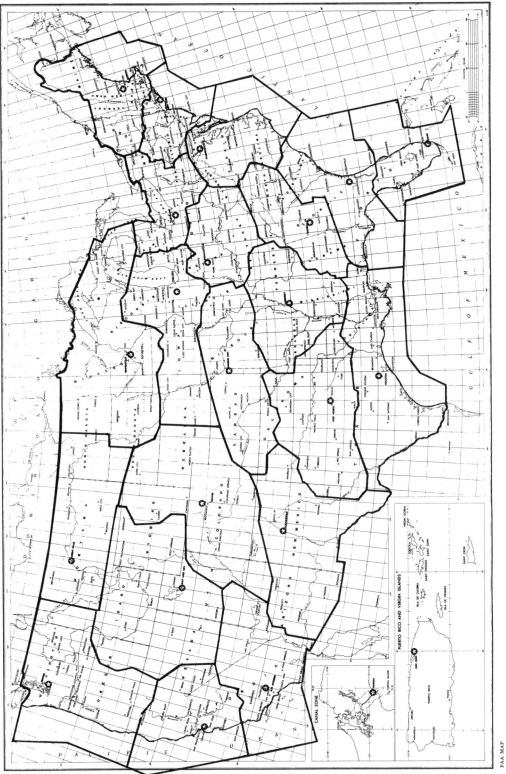

FAA MAP

Boundaries of the 21 adjoining control Centers in the United States. Other Centers are in Alaska (2), Hawaii, Guam, Puerto Rico and the Canal Zone.

Washington Center, the Chicago Center, the Indianapolis Center, the Los Angeles Center, and so on. Their radar control rooms are usually located in small, windowless one-story buildings out in the open country, some distance from the cities for which they are named. Each Center gets its radar signals from a number of antennas some hundreds of miles away. For example, all the New York Center radarscopes at Ronkonkomo, Long Island, get their signals from four antennas, one at the Kennedy airport, others in eastern and western Pennsylvania, and a fourth in southern New Jersey. These radar signals are transmitted to the Center by microwave similar to that used by the telephone company to transmit calls, in many places. However, special cables to improve reception are on the way. Controllers complain that weather or atmospheric conditions make radar temperamental and cause "bad days" when performance is poor.

For convenience each Center's airspace is divided into thirty to forty Sectors, irregularly shaped areas usually corresponding to the air traffic patterns in their part of the country. Each Sector is monitored by at least one radarscope, but in some cases an airspace is split in two horizontally and watched by *two* controllers. For example, one man may be watching the space *below* 15,000 feet while another man takes care of the airspace *above* 15,000 feet. This is done only in very congested areas. Sectors vary greatly in size. Some cover as much as forty square miles, others only ten or fifteen.

FAA Centers handle what is called *enroute* traffic—that is planes passing through. Some of these planes are on their way to or from a nearby airport, others are on their way from one distant city to another. With planes flying nonstop from New York to Honolulu or from Los Angeles to London, enroute controllers talk to quite a variety of pilots. They give these men the latest local weather forecasts and sometimes permission to change flight plans when pilots request this.

Centers do not handle terminal traffic, that is landings

What a pilot sees as he is coming
in for a landing at O'Hare Airport
in Chicago. Bottom photograph
shows the runway just before the
wheels touch down.

CHICAGO CENTER LOW

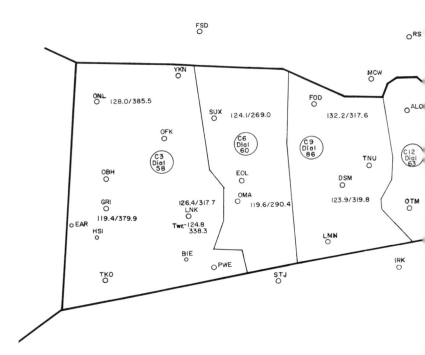

Map of the Chicago Center with the Sectors indicated by fine lines. O'Hare Airport in Chicago is indicated by letters ORD, near middle of right half of map (near *A7 Dial 25*). MKG (upper right hand corner) is Muskegon Airport. Omaha, Neb., is at extreme left, just south of symbol *C3 Dial 58*. These *Dial* notations are land-line telephone numbers of controllers covering the area. Other numbers, such as 128.2/317.6, are radio phone frequencies. First number is for pilots to reach controllers on very high frequency. Number after dash is ultrahigh frequency for the military.

ALTITUDE SECTORS and FREQ.

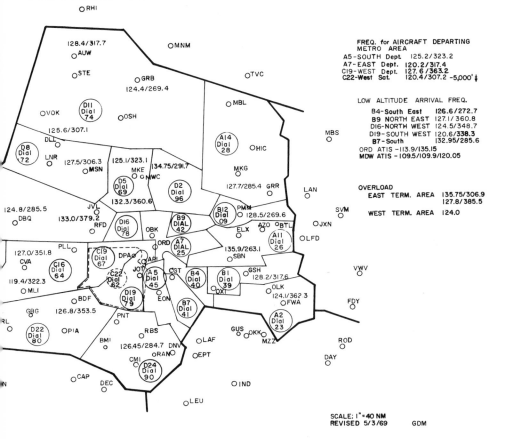

○ RHI

128.4/317.7
○ AUW
○ MNM

○ STE
○ GRB
124.4/269.4
○ TVC

DII Dial 74
○ VOK
○ OSH
○ MBL

125.6/307.1
DLL
○ A14 Dial 28
○ HIC
MBS ○

D8 Dial 72
LNR ○
127.5/306.3 ○ MSN
125.1/323.1
134.75/291.7
MKE ○ ○ NWC
MKG ○

D5 Dial 69
132.3/360.6
D2 Dial 96
127.7/285.4 GRR ○
LAN ○

124.8/285.5
○ DBQ
133.0/379.2 RFD
DI6 Dial 78
OBK ○
B12 Dial 09
PMM ○ 128.5/269.6
SVM ○
○ JXN

127.0/351.8
CVA ○
PLL ○
CI9 Dial 67
DPA ○
A7 DIAL 25
135.9/263.1
SBN ○
AZO ○ BTL
ELX ○
A11 Dial 26
○ LFD

CI6 Dial 64
C22 Dial 62
JOT ○
A5 Dial 45
CGT ○
B4 Dial 40
B1 Dial 39
GSH ○
128.2/317.6
○ VWV

119.4/322.3
○ MLI
○ BDF
DI9 Dial 79
EON ○
OX1 ○
OLK ○
124.1/362.3
○ FWA
FDY ○

GBG ○
126.8/353.5
PNT
B7 Dial 41
A2 Dial 23
ROD ○

D22 Dial 80
○ OPIA
BMI ○
RBS ○
126.45/284.7 DNV
○ LAF
GUS ○ ○ KK
MZZ ○
DAY ○

○ CAP
DEC ○
CMI ○
D24 Dial 90
○ RANO
○ EPT
○ IND

○ LEU

FREQ. for AIRCRAFT DEPARTING
METRO AREA
A5-SOUTH Dept.   125.2/323.2
A7-EAST Dept.   120.2/317.4
C19-WEST Dept.   127.6/363.2
C22-West Sat.   120.4/307.2 -5,000'‡

LOW ALTITUDE ARRIVAL FREQ.
B4-South East   126.6/272.7
B9 NORTH EAST   127.1/360.8
D16-NORTH WEST   124.5/348.7
D19-SOUTH WEST   120.6/338.3
B7-South   132.95/285.6
ORD ATIS -113.9/135.15
MDW ATIS -109.5/109.9/120.05

OVERLOAD
EAST TERM. AREA   135.75/306.9
                  127.8/385.5
WEST TERM. AREA   124.0

SCALE: 1"= 40 NM
REVISED 5/3/69   GDM

FEDERAL AVIATION ADMINISTRATION

and takeoffs, except occasionally to help out a small, nearby airport that has no control tower. There are a good many more such small airports around than most people who use the regular commercial flights realize. Some of these have neither tower nor radar nor radio and often only a short asphalt runway. However, controllers in the centers keep an eye on the planes that use them. And in an emergency these small airfields may be lifesavers for big commercial flights.

Often controllers find themselves talking to five or six pilots at once on the same wavelength and the situation gets impossible, so then they say very distinctly EVERY-BODY PLEASE MAINTAIN RADIO SILENCE UNTIL I CALL YOU, and then they call the pilots to come in, one at a time. While a controller usually has a choice of several frequencies for radio talk, he very seldom uses more than one.

The FAA has charge of the traffic at airports, where the terminal controllers work, handling takeoffs and arrivals. These men have the most complicated jobs of all. When a plane is coming in for a landing the last enroute controller at the nearby Center gives it a handoff to one of the airport radar control men in the IFR room. And before the plane finally rolls to a stop just outside the passenger building, it will have been handled by three or four controllers. It may, for example have been handed off to an additional controller for a few minutes between the Center's man and the final approach controller at the airport.

Bringing planes down is the most critical job controllers and pilots face, for it is here that most accidents happen. During a rush period when planes are touching down on a runway almost at the rate of one a minute, a controller can see the blips lining up on his scope many miles away. When everything runs smoothly, one pair of blips after another reaches a certain point just above the runway and then disappears, indicating that the plane has landed and is out of radar range.

But sometimes things don't go so smoothly. A captain

following all the correct procedures looks down and sees that the plane which landed just ahead of him has not yet cleared the runway. Maybe the taxi strip to the passenger area was still crowded with previous arrivals. Somebody along the line was just a few seconds too slow. The pilot about to land pulls his plane up and gives the engines a short burst of power to climb a few hundred feet out of the way. This is an MA, or missed approach, and there is a standard procedure to take care of it. The plane, still very low but now high enough to clear all the airport structures, goes straight ahead into an empty tunnel of airspace purposely kept clear at the end of every runway. Unless the

A heavy rain or snowfall makes trouble for controllers, showing up on scopes as white splotches.
CREIGHTON PEET

controller tells him otherwise he will make a sharp left turn after a certain number of seconds, and then another sharp left, and go back some little distance and get into the lineup of planes again. However, things may be so tight that the controller will give him other directions.

During a critical rush-hour congestion controllers seem to be hypnotized, living in a world of their own. Long training has made many of their reactions instinctive and automatic. They speak quietly but very rapidly into their head phones, pencil brief notations on their Flight Progress Strips, shift nervously around their scopes on their rolling chairs, listen intently to the pilots of distant planes, and always, always keep their eyes glued to the little slashes of light on their scopes. An outsider listening in on the steady stream of talk between a controller and half a dozen pilots is baffled. Not only do they use their own special words—usually abbreviations—but a controller can switch from Pan Am to BOAC to Eastern to Air France to Delta without catching his breath, giving each pilot exact directions for his particular situation. Then there will be maybe twenty seconds of silence, while each of the blips on the scope crawls a little farther along, until the rapid-fire talk resumes. There's no nonsense about coffee breaks or lunch or dinner, often for hours at a time. In really busy airports a couple of hours overtime several times a week in the radar control rooms are taken for granted, as well as a six-day week.

The VFR (Visual Flight Rules) takeoff controllers live in a different world, almost an outdoor world. They work in the glass-enclosed "bubble" at the top of the airport's control tower, called the "cab." While they do have radar, a great deal of the time in clear weather they can look out over the airport, and sometimes using binoculars, see the lineup of planes on the takeoff runways, waiting for them to give the word that will send them on their way. At the same time they can see arrivals slowing down and taxying to the passenger terminals. At many airports, including Kennedy and Los Angeles International, takeoff controllers also have big TV screens, called "bright displays," about the size of an ordinary TV screen, which magnify a radar view of a runway. They can be seen perfectly in full daylight. Even at night the lineup of planes is usually clearly visible to the controllers in the cab.

The expansion of airport passenger terminals constantly threatens to cut off these clear views of runways from the controllers in the cab, but FAA regulations are very specific on this point. No buildings can interfere with the sightlines from the cab. However, as things get more complicated at airports, electronic signaling devices are being installed so that controllers can tell where all planes are at all times.

Finally, one after another the local (takeoff) controllers give captains clearance to roll down a runway and roar into a takeoff.

All major aircraft control positions, either in airports or Centers, or high up in the cab, are manned twenty-four hours a day every day in the year, winter, summer, weekends and holidays. Only some of the smaller VFR towers are run on a sixteen-hour day. There can never be an instant without controllers' watching our airspace. Air travel and air cargo movements have replaced so much of our railroad traffic and ocean transport that they are essential in keeping the country running. The airplane is now as essential to us as the air through which it flies.

Getting
Cleared
for
Takeoff

Before a plane lifts off a runway there are a good many necessary formalities involving not only the plane's crew but a series of local controllers. At this point these men first accept responsibility for the radar surveillance of a plane and its safe separation from other aircraft, and then they hand it off to the first of what may be a long chain of other controllers in radar rooms all around the world.

In preparing for a flight, the captain first of all reports to the airline's office at the airport and consults the flight plan that has been generated for him by the computer. One might think that in flying to the same cities two or three times a week a pilot would always take the same route and wouldn't need a special flight plan each time. But the computer's flight plan takes many things into account and may differ considerably from the FAA's "Preferred Route." Basically, the computer decides how the plane can reach its destination in the shortest possible flying time, which is more

In an airport office, before taking
off, an airline captain consults
weather reports and the computer-
generated flight plan for this particular flight.

important than taking the route with the shortest mileage.
To do this the computer takes into account the make of
plane involved and its characteristics, the weather forecast,
possible storm conditions, the present location of the jet
stream, and any turbulance—even clear air turbulance—that
may have been reported by other pilots in the last few hours,
and many other factors.

The powerful current of air called the jet stream moves
generally west to east, so a plane flying from Los Angeles
to New York can often pick up a tail wind that may give
it an additional hundred miles per hour of speed in certain
areas. On the other hand, a plane flying west from New
York may go many miles out of its way to avoid the jet

stream, which would slow it down. The jet stream is why it usually takes about an hour longer to fly from Europe to America than it takes to go the other way. It is not practical to avoid the jet stream entirely on such a long flight. The computer uses all these factors and many others in reaching its decision.

If the captain accepts the computer's flight plan—although he does not have to and does not always do so—he contacts the ARTC (Air Route Traffic Control) section of the FAA, either by phone or teletype, and gets an OK for his flight. Any changes in route a captain makes are usually minor and cause no problems. Later, any changes the captain feels necessary when he is in flight must be cleared with the nearest enroute controller.

Next, the Captain picks up his "brainbag," his bulky, satchel-like briefcase, and starts for his plane, accompanied by his copilot and engineer. This bag is loaded with all the maps he might ever need, and all the latest bulletins and orders issued by his airline and the FAA.

While the FAA furnishes pilots of both airlines and private

Computer room in the Los Angeles Center at Palmdale, Calif. In such rooms alphanumerics data is stored on tapes.

On his way to his plane a captain
is loaded down with his "brainbag," a jumbo briefcase filled with
maps and company and FAA bulletins.

planes with a complete set of Flight Information Maps printed by the U. S. Coast and Geodetic Survey, most airlines use supplemental maps made by the Jeppesen Company of Denver, Colorado. While these maps are based on the ones printed by the Government, they have additional information applying to particular airlines. Some of these maps cover an airline's complete route from one city to another, while others are quite small and fit into small notebooks. A map may, for instance, show only an airport's layout, in great detail, such as the latest changes in runways, and note any under repair, as well as new airport construction and other features that might affect an approach. All FAA and airlines maps are kept up to date and some are reprinted every two or three months.

Once in the cockpit—or flight deck as some call it—the captain, copilot and engineer start running through the first of the several printed checklists covering all of the plane's electrical and mechanical systems that must be checked before takeoff. This is a serious process required by both the FAA and the airline. Usually the engineer reads off the items while the captain and copilot push switches and levers and inspect signal lights that indicate operation. Soon the passengers are all aboard, the doors are closed, the engines are started, and the plane leaves the gate and is on its way. Then the following sequence starts.

1. As he moves away from the gate, the captain contacts the visual ground controller sitting high up in the cab on the top of the airport's tower and asks for a clearance to taxi out to the runway.

2. This ground controller, who can usually see a plane with the naked eye, but certainly with binoculars, then calls ARTC and says, for instance, that TWA 345 is taxiing out to the runway, and asks if they have clearance for takeoff. Right away ARTC comes back saying that everything is OK and that TWA 345 is cleared for such-and-such a route. Immediately this information is relayed to the plane's captain by the ground controller.

Before takeoff, the flight engineer reads a long list of items to the captain and his copilot to make sure all systems are functioning properly.

High up in his cab at the Los Angeles control tower, a controller follows planes visually, often using binoculars.

3. But this isn't all. Everything must be double-checked. The captain, who copied his clearance down in writing when he heard it read to him, now reads its exact wording back to the ground controller. And since all controller-pilot talk is automatically recorded on tapes in an airport, everything is now official.

4. By now the plane is lined up ready for takeoff on the runway, all of the checklists have been gone over, and the captain is only waiting for word for the ground controller that there is an adequate separation (distance from the plane ahead of him), and that it is his turn to take off.

5. About this time the visual ground controller in the cab gives a handoff of the plane to the ground departure controller—also in the cab—and then, as soon as the plane is airborne, it is handed off to the radar departure controller in the airport IFR room. Soon a controller in the nearest Center assumes control and starts it on its way.

Crossing the Country

Planes flying across country, and even across the continent without stopping, of course deal only with the enroute controllers in the Centers. Since some nonstop flights (such as those from New York to Honolulu, Chicago to Mexico City, and Los Angeles over the Pole to London) often last eight or nine hours or more, the voices of controllers in their radar rooms scattered all over the map, reaching up from thousands of feet below, are a welcome contact for the men up there on the flight deck of a jetliner. They get a chance to talk shop and pick up ball scores and top news, as well as the latest weather reports. In time pilots and controllers get to recognize each other's voices and become friends, although they may never see each other.

Suppose a plane takes off from Denver to fly to New York. As it leaves the Denver Airport it will first be watched by the airport's visual controller in the glass-enclosed cab at the top of the tower, then by the airport's radar con-

27

A big radar control room such as this one in the Indianapolis Center is filled with a variety of electronic devices.

Controllers inspect experimental equipment. Twenty-four-hour clock at upper left indicates time is 19–38.

trollers. But very shortly a controller in the Denver Center located in Longmont, Colorado, about forty-five miles from Denver, will get a handoff of this plane from the airport's departure controller and will pick up the blips representing the plane on his scope. Now this plane is the Center's responsibility, and it will pass from one Sector controller to another until it reaches the eastern limits of the Denver Center's airspace, somewhere near the middle of Kansas. In this time it will have been guided by about six controllers in the Denver Center. The last man here will give a handoff of the plane to a Sector in the Kansas City Center located at Olathe, Kansas, which will hand it off to one Sector after another until it reaches the eastern limits of the Kansas City Center. It will then get a handoff to the Indiana Center

Shrimp boats show up clearly on this unusual setup. Double scopes, one installed vertically, one horizontally, are more or less experimental.

LOS ANGELES DEPT. OF AIRPORTS

at Indianapolis, the Cleveland Center at Oberlin, Ohio, and finally the New York Center at Ronkonkoma, Long Island, where it will be handed to the approach controllers at La Guardia or J. F. Kennedy Airport, who will bring it down.

Around New York, Washington and Chicago, Centers have many small Sectors, and so more controllers handling a plane passing through, than such Western states as Colorado.

Very often controllers sitting next to each other at a Center are covering adjacent Sectors of airspace, and when they handoff a plane to each other, they do just that— reach out and hand over the plane's Flight Strip in its little plastic holder. However, if the next controller to handle this plane is in another part of the room, an assistant controller will take it to him. If the plane is on its way to another Center, the computer will transmit the information to that Center.

Parking
Lots
in
The
Sky

Motor traffic entering a city on a congested highway often has to slow down or even stop entirely for long periods of time, but a plane coming in for a landing at a crowded airport can't do this. It has to operate a little above what is called its "stall speed," just to stay airborne. Usually this is about 280 miles per hour, but the plane must move faster at higher altitudes where the air is thinner.

When a great number of planes are heading for an airport and want to land about the same time, and the air approach corridors are filled with aircraft even many miles from the airport, the controllers in the Center send new arrivals to aerial parking lots called "holding patterns." These are sections of airspace, sometimes fifty or sixty miles from the airport, in which planes can circle around and around in a race-track-shaped oval pattern, stacked one above the other, exactly one thousand feet apart. The exactness of this "separation" is extremely important because there are sometimes twenty or even twenty-five planes in the same holding pattern at different levels.

Stacking usually starts around 9,000 feet for jets and 4,000 feet for prop planes. The second plane sent to a jet area goes in at an altitude of 10,000 feet, and the next at the 11,000 foot level, and so on up, usually to around 21,000 feet, or higher. Holding patterns come in different sizes for different types of planes. Small private prop planes may be sent to an area that is about five miles long and two miles wide. A big jetliner will go into a holding pattern that may be as much as thirty-six miles long and twenty miles wide. If things are really bad and the controller finds he is getting more traffic than he can handle, he may, for a short time, cut the separation from 1,000 feet to 500. However, this is done only in an emergency situation and must immediately be reported to FAA supervisors as a "system deviation."

Naturally a Center controller doesn't wait until a plane is close to an airport and ready to line up for a landing approach before he sends it into a holding pattern. When it is still many miles away, he tells the captain he will have to go to such and such a holding area, entering at, say, the 14,000-foot level. Holding areas around the Kennedy-LaGuardia-Newark complex have such names as South Gate, Bohemia, Broadway, Carmel, Princeton, and Deer Park. When the captain gets the word he immediately heads for the assigned area, cutting down his speed as much as possible, since he is just killing time.

Center controllers send planes to holding areas, but airport controllers take them out, because they know when they will have space to handle a new arrival. When an airport controller finds that he can land another plane, he tells the Center controller he is ready to accept another aircraft. Then the Center controller advises the pilot of the plane at the bottom of one of the stacks to switch to the airport's radio phone frequency, so that he can prepare to land.

However, this may be complicated, because this is a busy

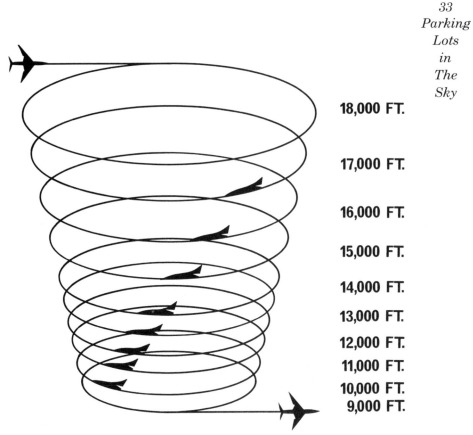

18,000 FT.

17,000 FT.

16,000 FT.

15,000 FT.

14,000 FT.

13,000 FT.

12,000 FT.

11,000 FT.

10,000 FT.
9,000 FT.

ELLEN WILLIAMS

Diagram shows eight planes circling in a holding pattern, plus
one leaving at the bottom, and
another entering at the top.

area. The pilot often has to take a roundabout route to get
his plane into the proper lineup, climbing high above some
planes crossing his path, and "tunneling" under others,
just as one automobile highway passes under another on
the ground. This is why some big airports have special controllers who do nothing but work on planes leaving a holding pattern.

After the bottom plane has left a stack, leaving the bottom
position in the stack empty, the airport controller starts
"laddering the planes down," first telling the Number 2

pilot to come down 1,000 feet and then, a few seconds later, telling the pilot of the No. 3 plane to also come down 1,000 feet, and so on, all the way up to the man at the top of the stack. When *he* moves out, the top space is empty, so the airport controller calls the Center man on a "land line" (regular telephone) and tells him this space is available if a new plane shows up needing a holding area.

Most major airports have a number of holding areas, and O'Hare in Chicago has 14, some as far north as Racine and halfway to Milwaukee, and others as far south as Joliet. In the New York City area, Kennedy, LaGuardia and Newark each have three holding areas scattered between Princeton, New Jersey and Stamford, Connecticut. In the Los Angeles area, where there are many small airports, there are seven holding areas from six to fifty miles away from the big Los Angeles International Airport, some of which are over the Pacific.

Above the regular holding patterns there are sometimes "High Altitude Delay Absorbing Patterns," which start at around 23,000 feet and go on up to 39,000 feet. Above 18,000 feet altitudes are referred to as Flight Levels, and (for instance) Flight Level one nine zero is actually 19,000 feet.

But while some controllers have been busy sending new arrivals to fill up all the holding areas around an airport, others have been calling first nearby and then distant Centers to warn them that they cannot accept any more traffic for a while, or possibly "only one plane every five minutes."

This refusal of new traffic starts when the controllers see their scopes being dangerously jammed with planes. Their coordinators then are put to work.

If things look very bad for the next two or three hours, the backup may reach thousands of miles. In the case of a tieup at Kennedy, planes about to take off for New York from Seattle or Los Angeles may be held up for an hour— or two, or three. A new computer center in Kansas City will one day keep all airports and Centers informed of logjams anywhere, so that traffic will flow more smoothly—at least everybody hopes so.

Meanwhile, back in the holding patterns on the East Coast, passengers are fussing and fuming and telling each other how many important appointments they are missing, and the pilots up front are keeping a sharp eye on their fuel supplies. Pilots are absolutely forbidden to leave a holding pattern except in the case of an extreme emergency.

The pilot of a circling aircraft may finally have to call the controller and say his fuel is running low. If he adds, "I've got just about enough to make my alternate," he gets permission to leave the holding pattern. What the Captain means is that he has just about enough fuel to reach an alternate airport, which in the case of New York might be Boston or Philadelphia or Montreal, or even Chicago or Bermuda! Also, when he says he has "just enough" fuel to make one of those airports, he means that he also has enough fuel to spend about an hour in one of that other airport's holding patterns, waiting for a chance to land.

In summer a pilot may have several choices (specified when he filed his flight plan before he took off), but in winter, Boston, Montreal or Chicago may be fighting a blizzard and working desparately to clear three or four feet of snow from the runways and don't want any drop-in visitors.

It has been estimated that planes spend about 150,000 hours a year in holding patterns waiting for clearance to land. When the holding pattern system was first put into use, some pilots and passengers, weary and impatient with circling around for an hour or two, invented "emergencies" that forced controllers to crowd things a little and take planes out of a stack for a landing ahead of others. But when it turned out after inspection that there was plenty of fuel and nothing whatever was wrong with the plane, FAA inspectors started checking all such planes carefully, even to measuring the fuel left in the tanks, and pilots were fined heavily if the emergency was not genuine. Today planes stay put in their holding patterns until called out by their controllers.

While controllers can of course see planes in a holding pattern on their scopes, they don't pay much attention to them until it comes time to bring one of them out, or unless a plane strays from the pattern through carelessness. Not long ago a pilot from a foreign airline circling in a Kennedy holding pattern suddenly realized that he was over Boston, and he had quite a little trouble getting back into his pattern, asking various controllers along the way for help.

At all times captains take things into their own hands when a bad thunderstorm comes up—even to leaving a holding pattern—which is strictly against the rules at other times. In order to circumnavigate a thunderstorm, or leave course, they should first request permission to deviate from established rules.

Ocean Control

The flight deck of a big airliner is a mass of dials, gauges, switches, blinking colored lights and mysterious little black boxes. The panels holding these controls and indicators reach from the floor in front of the pilot and copilot up to the ceiling and halfway across it. There is hardly room for the three or more officers seated around the big jet control throttles that push up from the middle of the floor.

At 30,000 to 40,000 feet above the Atlantic or Pacific, on the edge of space, the sunlight is blinding as it reflects from the blanket of white clouds far below. It pours in a big arc through the windows on three sides of the cockpit, and the pilot and copilot have sheets of green plastic hanging in front of them to cut down the glare. "Downstairs," as the crew speaks of the earth, it may be overcast, raining or snowing. But up here it is usually a dazzling, sunny day, with the outside temperature around thirty or forty degrees below zero. Storms seldom get this high.

As a plane flys east at 500 to 600 miles an hour, night changes into day with unbelievable speed. In a very few minutes it has left night and roared into broad daylight.

Many planes are equipped with an autopilot, an auto-

Radarscopes along the coast show few markings and little activity where they extend over the ocean. Again, controller has shrimp boat between his fingers. ACK-WACK is area just west of Nantucket, Mass.

CREIGHTON PEET

matic device that takes control of the plane and keeps it on course, so that for hours at a time the human pilots need to do little but check their instruments. At such a time flying a giant aircraft looks absurdly easy.

But there is the matter of making sure you are on course, and of reporting your position to the controllers back on land, maybe thousands of miles away. Planes traveling one of the regular aircraft lanes over the ocean to Europe—or Hawaii, Australia or Japan—must stay 120 miles apart horizontally and keep a vertical separation of 1000 feet if they are below 29,000 and 2,000 feet if they are above 29,000.

Every so often the captain or his navigator checks their position. Winds may change a plane's course slightly, and always the instruments must be checked for accuracy.

Of course there are no beacons or landmarks over the ocean, and regular land-based radar controllers can't follow planes more than about 125 or 150 miles out from the coast. And so there are pairs of unusual radarscopes clear at

Ocean control desk at the New York Center. No radarscopes here, only telephone connections to ARINC. Note some men are older; no big tensions build up here.

CREIGHTON PEET

the back of the big radar control room at the New York Center at Ronkonkomo, Long Island, and in a similar spot in the Oakland Center at Oakland, California. The screens of these radarscopes are half empty except for the circular mileage markings. This is because half of each scope reaches out over the ocean.

For the thousands of miles of ocean beyond the small areas covered by these coastal scopes, FAA controllers rely on a company called Aeronautical Radio, Inc., known to everybody simply as ARINC. This operates a vast two-way radio telephone network with transmitters in New York, Miami, San Juan, New Orleans, Seattle, San Francisco, Honolulu, Okinawa, to name some of the centers. Through its transmitters land-based controllers get, every hour, an accurate report on all the planes flying over the Atlantic and Pacific, as well as over the continental United States.

The New York ocean control area, covering 1,500,000 square miles of ocean, is divided into three "manual" sectors— that is, without radar. These reach from Gander, adjacent to Canadian Control on the north, down to San Juan, Puerto Rico, on the South, Santa Maria Control (Portuguese) on the east, and of course the Boston-New York-Washington-Jacksonville-Miami domestic radar control Centers on the west.

While controllers who cover the shoreline do use radar, none of the men in ocean control have radarscopes. They have only telephone headsets, which connect them with ARINC. When a plane calls in to give a report on its location, the ARINC operator dials a code number, which connects him with the controller watching the Sector in which the plane is now flying and reports the aircraft's position verbally or by teletype. Here the controller writes the plane's position on a flight strip for his area. The computer has produced as many as six or seven strips for each aircraft, for each Sector. These strips are posted by the controller at intervals of roughly five degrees of latitude or longitude—

about 300 miles apart—or at any special point at which there may be crossing traffic.

Between them, controllers along the Eastern Seaboard, in Boston, New York, Jacksonville, Miami, and other coastal cities, follow the movements of aircraft over some 1,500,000 square miles of the Atlantic through reports received by ARINC. But of course before a pilot can give his location he must determine, within three to five miles, where he is. Knowing his ground speed, the course he has been taking, and the time since his last calculation, a captain usually has a pretty good idea of about where he is, but flying at 35,000 feet above the Atlantic at 600 miles an hour he must have something specific to back up his hunch. So every time his plane has flown another ten degrees or so of longitude (going east or west), or latitude (going north or south) the captain gets to work.

The oldest and most common system used by planes, as well as ships, today is LORAN (short for "long range navi-

ARINC communications center in San Francisco keeps in contact with flights over the Pacific and informs land-based controllers of their positions.

AERONAUTICAL RADIO, INC.

Section of navigation chart of the North Atlantic for pilots using LORAN navigation beams. Letters and numbers close to beams identify them. Pilots who have tuned in on a beam can look at the chart and see where they are —after finding two beams that cross. For the landlubber, map is tricky, as it also has much additional information. Note such locations as "Tuna," "Haddock," and "Porpoise," far from any land.

FEDERAL AVIATION ADMINISTRATION

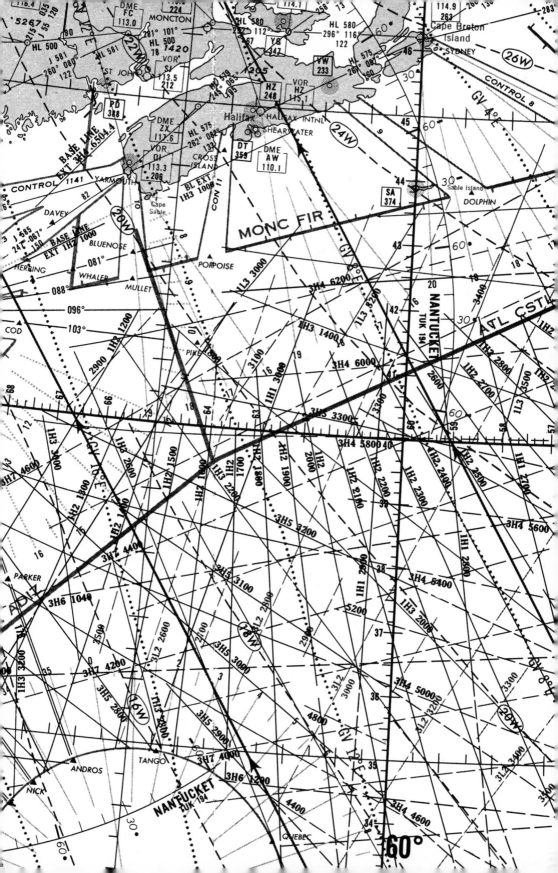

gation"). This is a system of pulsating beams sent out from more than eighty tall, slim towers located in many parts of the world. The path of the beams—each of which reaches about 600 miles (farther at night)—and the character or frequency of the beams, are printed in number form on a series of charts.

Using an oscilloscope and other equipment, a captain tunes in on a beam he thinks he should be near, using the frequency printed on the chart for that beam. It is very much like tuning in on a particular TV or radio station. It is helpful to find that he is near the beam, but of course that knowledge does not give him a definite location. Then he looks at his chart and picks another beam that intersects, or crosses, the first one. If he finds that he is also near the second beam, he knows he is near the point where they cross—which gives him his position.

These LORAN transmitters were all built by the United States during and after the Second World War, and many, including all on U.S. territory, are operated by the Coast Guard. Some others are now operated by the countries in which they are located. LORAN transmitters are very thin triangular steel towers from 200 or 300 to 1300 feet high, anchored down with a great many long cables reaching in all directions to keep from being blown over. About twenty men work at each LORAN station, making sure that the pulsating signal never fails and that the frequency is always correct for that location.

Life on a LORAN station is often lonely, for many of them are located on tiny islands far at sea. Usually one twelve-month tour of duty is about all a man can take.

A second navigation system used over the ocean is the Decca/Dectrop, which resembles LORAN in that it also uses transmissions from groups of land stations. It has a very unusual feature, however—a small display map of the area being covered by the flight. As the plane flies, this small map unrolls, and a "cursor," or pointer, shows exactly where the plane is. For ocean flights this map shows only longi-

Flight deck of a Pan Am 747. *1.* Front instrument console facing pilot and copilot. *2.* Flight engineer's panel through which he controls jets. *3.* Closeup of controls, showing location of the Carousel IV inertial navigation systems. For safety, the 747 carries three complete sets of these instruments.

Control console on Pan Am's Boeing 707 with inertial navigation instruments installed on either side of radarscope (white buttons). Very similar to the last picture but a little clearer and a more commonplace and better-known plane.

tude and latitude markings, useful to a pilot in reporting his position.

Then there is the Doppler Navigation System, a British invention (also made in the United States by Bendix), which has the advantage of being entirely self-contained and requiring no land stations. It is all packed neatly into six small black boxes in the cockpit plus a thin antenna fastened rigidly to the outside of the aircraft. It operates by continuously sending four radar beams to the surface of the ocean. The beams are pointed down and out, at angles, to form a rectangle. By measuring the fraction of a second it takes the beams to bounce back to the antenna on the plane, the computer calculates how fast the plane is going, how far it has gone, how much off course it has drifted and in what direction. With all this information it is easy to find out where a plane is at any time. Although Doppler is marvelously efficient over the ocean, it has been discovered that it does not work over a relatively smooth body of water, such as a lake. Doppler needs rough water to operate. Over a lake in fair weather it "locks on" to a single position and gives no further reading.

Pilots and airlines also think very highly of inertial navigation systems, similar to those used by submarines to navigate under water. These systems are also self-contained; that is, they require no land transmitters. For inertial guidance a series of extremely sensitive gyroscopes, or rapidly spinning wheels, like tops, along with a small computer, are mounted in the cockpit in four little black boxes weighing altogether about fifty pounds. These power-driven gyroscopes are started spinning before the plane leaves the ground. After that, *any movement of the plane in any direction* is registered by the gyros, and the distance and direction in which the plane has moved are recorded by the computer. Even hours later, after thousands of miles of flight, this device will show accurately a plane's altitude, as well as how far it has gone and in which direction. As a test of what inertial navigation can do, one manufacturer, AC Electronics,

These little black boxes aren't very dramatic, but they do a fantastic job. Fitted into the control panel of a plane, this inertial navigation Carousel IV System shows a pilot exactly where he is even after hours of flight.

Inside the little boxes are delicate gyroscopes and accelerometers, which provide the signals to keep a plane on course. Six-inch rule shows exact size of gyros.

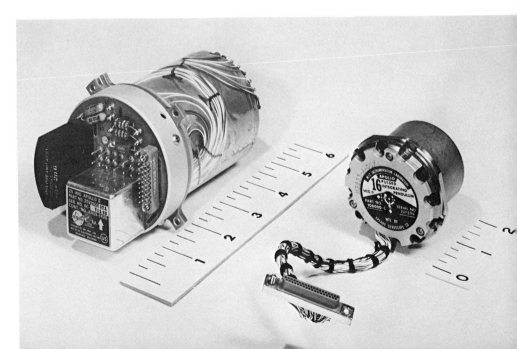

a division of General Motors, mounted its Carousel IV Navigation System on one of the new 747 superjets. This was then flown nonstop from Seattle, Washington, to Le Bourget Airfield, near Paris. During most of that nine-hour flight, the inertial system was hooked up to the plane's autopilot, and between them the two devices flew the plane nearly 4,000 miles, or from Seattle to near the English coast, ending up only 8.8 miles off course.

A fifth means of finding an aircraft's location is to "shoot the sun" as captains do at sea, standing on the bridges of their ships. Actually, pilots can use their sextants to find where they are by also setting them on the moon or stars at any time of the day or night. In a modern plane a tube from the sextant must project through the roof of the cockpit to the outside of the plane. Since planes are highly pressurized today, this tube must go through an airlock so that no pressure is lost. "Human navigation," as this is called, is still used a great deal in some parts of the world, especially in the South Pacific, where LORAN does not operate.

At this time most commercial planes in the United States use a combination of LORAN and Doppler, checking one against the other.

However he finds his position, a pilot reports it to ARINC by radio phone, and this information is relayed to his land-based controller, who makes a record of his location and the time. If at any other time the controller or the airline's office wants to contact a pilot, he can be reached by calling the plane's special four-letter code call known as SELCAL. Every commercial plane has its own code number, which might be compared to a phone number.

Suppose a BOAC executive in London or a PAN AM executive in New York or a controller with an important weather forecast wants to reach a plane during an ocean flight. He calls the local ARINC office, where the operator, using this plane's code, puts in a call. In a few seconds the Captain sees a light flashing in his cockpit, and soon he finds himself talking to a controller, or to his boss in London or New

As can be seen, only three of the many planes on this scope are equipped to produce alphanumeric signals. However, three more, whose alphanumeric tags are stored at the bottom left, are due shortly. When the planes they represent come near the airport (JFK) they will slide over and attach themselves to them. Large figures at top indicate the time is 14–12, or 2:12 P.M.

CREIGHTON PEET

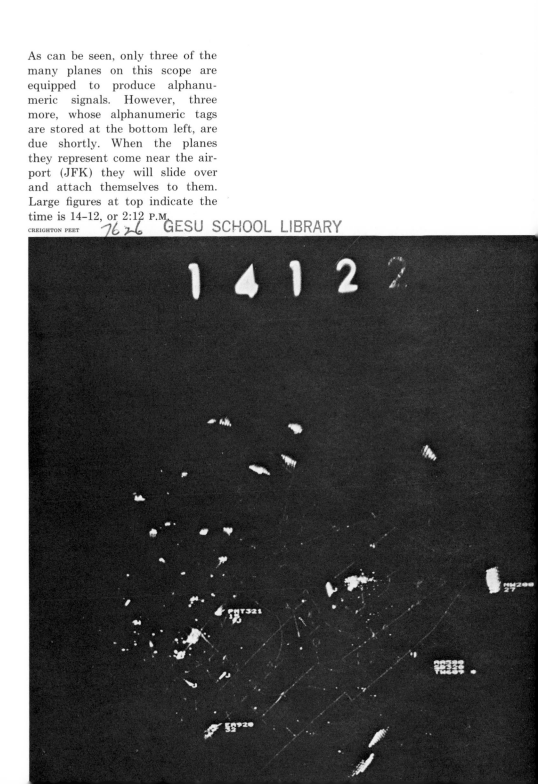

York. All British SELCAL codes start with a "B," and French ones with an "F," while American codes are made up of a variety of letters and numbers.

Pilots and controllers all over the world use English to talk to each other, Greenwich Mean Time (GMT)—or, as U.S. controllers call it, *Zulu Time*—and of course the 24-hour clock used by the military.

This way, when it is 5:45 in the afternoon in the eastern United States, it is 17:45 for people in aviation. But when it is 2:45 PM in Los Angeles, it is still 17:45 for pilots and controllers in California as well as in New York, London, Rome and New Delhi. We use Zulu Time because it is specific and definite and is never confused by time zones, daylight saving or anything else. Written, the above times would appear as 17:45Z.

All around the world aircraft controllers work very much as they do in America, but in Europe there is something called Eurocontrol which covers about half a dozen countries, although each country supports the control centers within its boundaries.

Controller-
Pilot
Talk

The skies above us are filled with all kinds of electronic talk besides TV and radio programs. All day and until after midnight, for instance, about 4,000 controllers and the captains of some 2,000 commerical jets and countless private planes are talking almost continuously as they take off from runways, roar from city to city, often at around 35,000 feet, and finally settle on landing strips hundreds or even thousands of miles away. At every crucial moment during these flights controllers have been offering advice and information by radio phone.

But vital as is this talk between controllers and pilots, it is baffling and only rarely makes any sense to the average listener. Sometimes these men have brief, chatty moments, but most of their talk consists of a series of numbers, abbreviations, and special made-up terms which have been developed over the years. The need to be specific and absolutely sure you understand correctly what you have heard results in a great deal of repetition, and frequently captains repeat a controller's instructions with only a slightly different wording.

Foreign captains, while speaking English well enough, often have heavy accents and different ways of saying things, and a controller has to be smart as well as quick to understand their meanings. Fortunately, a great deal of the time both instructions and responses are fairly routine.

Most of all, talk is very, very fast—so fast that often one man starts before the other has finished. The information the controller gives him is vital to a captain. He is operating four monstrous jet engines that are driving him through the trackless air at 400 to 600 miles an hour. There's no pausing to think or to decide which course he might take. Neither the captain nor the controller ever forgets that the air all around that plane is swarming with other equally powerful and dangerous aircraft.

The following conversations were taken from tapes made at Kennedy Airport and are exactly as recorded by the FAA except for the addition of a few connecting words to make them easier to understand. As you can see, a controller often switches back and forth between a number of planes—a little like a juggler keeping three or four balls in the air at once. "G.C." means ground control; that is, a controller speaking. The other voices are identified by abbreviations for the airlines, such as are given below in italics:

G.C.   *Ten twenty-one* ident——
             Seven ten tango kilo left turn heading two sixty
             Ten twenty-one continue present heading another thirty seconds I'll have instructions for you shortly

Pilot   OK

                 [*This plane is what controllers call an "itinerant"—that is, a private plane. In this case the owner has chosen to call his craft* TEN TWENTY-ONE SEVEN TEN TANGO KILO.

> *This is like the man who calls his boat*
> MARY LOU *or* SALLY B.]

G.C.	*Eastern fifty-five* ident again——
EAL	*Eastern fifty-five* identing
G.C.	*Eastern fifty-five* descend and maintain three thousand, report when you leave six
EAL	OK leaving nine for three, will report leaving six
G.C.	Roger

> [*Controller asked for a second identification,*
> *that is a second transponder-produced*
> *showing on his scope*]

G.C.	Okay *Clipper seventy-nine* squawk ident
PAA	Identing *number seventy-nine*
G.C.	*Clipper seventy-nine* maintain two hundred knots —descend to nine thousand
PAA	*Clipper seventy-nine* maintain two hundred knots descending to nine thousand out of ten
G.C.	Roger *Trans World one,* ident again
TWA1	Descend to nine *TWA one.* We're out of eleven thousand now
G.C.	Roger
G.C.	*Shamrock five three five* descend and maintain one two thousand
S535	Roger *five thirty-five* is out of one three zero to one two zero
G.C.	Roger

> [*Irish International Airlines has come down*
> *1,000 feet, from 13,000 to 12,000.*]

G.C.	*Eastern two two nine* descend and maintain one three thousand
EA229	Out of one four, for one three *Eastern two twenty-nine*
G.C.	*Clipper seventy-nine* descend and maintain three thousand, report leaving six

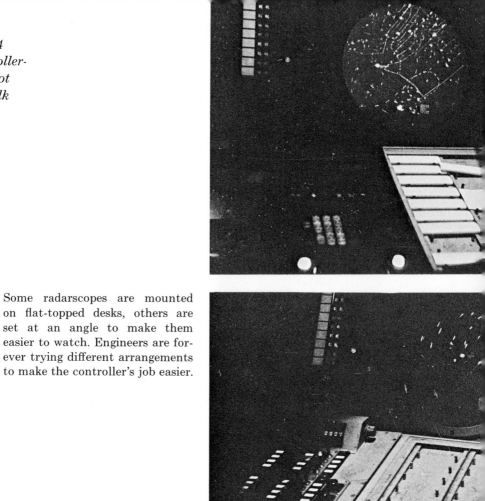

Some radarscopes are mounted on flat-topped desks, others are set at an angle to make them easier to watch. Engineers are forever trying different arrangements to make the controller's job easier.

CREIGHTON PEET

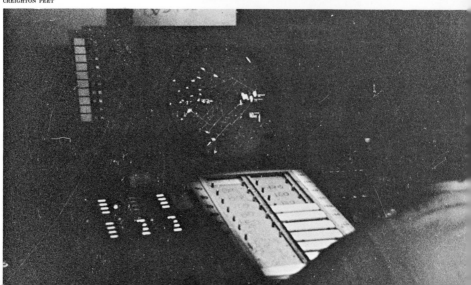

PAA   We're out of nine. *Clipper seventy-nine* is cleared to three

G.C.   Roger

G.C.   *Clipper one zero three* descend and maintain one four thousand

G.C.   *Roger Trans World three eight zero one* descend and maintain one five thousand

TWA3801   *Trans-World three eight zero one* is out of one six zero for one five zero [*He has left 16,000 for 15,000.*]

G.C.   Roger

> [*In this last exchange two Pan Am planes and one Trans World were all taken care of in a hurry*]

G.C.   [*Who has obviously been having trouble getting a squawk ident on his scope.*]
I'm still not getting anything on the ident feature. What is your airspeed now? Try one more ident, please [*silence*]

G.C.   *TWA* sir, are you identing?

TWA   Yes, I am [*meaning he has pushed transponder button*]

G.C.   Yeah, I guess it's just not working. Just turn off your transponder, please. I have your radar contact, but I'm not getting any ident off it. Maintain three thousand

> [*In the following exchange the controller gives the pilot a "squawk code zero three zero zero"; this is the code given to this plane on this flight and enables this plane's blips to attach themselves to the correct data tags on the face of the scope when the alphanumerics system is used.*]

G.C.   *Air Canada six twenty-four* squawk code zero three zero zero

AC624	*Air Canada six twenty-four*
G.C.	*Air Canada six twenty-four* proceed direct to Deer Park VOR depart Deer Park on two two eight radial for vectors final approach course thirty-one ILS
AC624	Roger direct Deer Park depart Deer Park two two eight radial for vectors six twenty-four desired speed?
G.C.	Ah—Squawk ident *Air Canada six twenty-four* squawk ident once more
AC624	'kay
G.C.	Two twenty knots for *Air Canada*
AC624	Roger *six twenty-four*

[Deer Park is a major holding pattern area for Kennedy Airport, but its nearby VOR (Visual Omni Range), a navigation beacon, is useful as identification. The Omni Range is one with 360 degrees, so the two two eight radial would be about where the hand of a clock would be at about twenty minutes after the hour. This is the direction the controller is telling the pilot to take. On maps all Omni Ranges are zeroed on the magnetic North.]

Controller instructions to pilots taking off are usually fairly standard and quite brief. After all, within a minute or so these planes will be handed off to the Center controller, who will really start them on their way.

G.C.	*KLM six two two* climb and maintain flight level two four zero (2,400) [feet] squawk code two one
KLM622	Flight level two four zero code twenty-one
G.C.	*TWA eight zero one* turn left heading zero four zero climb and maintain flight level two four zero
TWA801	Roger zero four zero and climb to two four zero

G.C.   *KLM six two two* contact New York Center radar on one two six point eight [a radio frequency]

G.C.   *Trans World eight zero one*—you have traffic at one o'clock westbound

> [*When a controller wants to warn a pilot he is too near another aircraft he tells him he "has traffic"; one o'clock of course means just to the right of straight ahead or where the figure one would be if you were looking straight at the figure 12 on a clock.*]

G.C.   *National six zero one* turn right heading one siz zero and squawk code twenty-one

NAT601   Twenty-one—what was heading?

G.C.   One six zero for *National six zero one* [*Tricky, this!*]

G.C.   *National seventy-nine* squawk one one zero zero

NAT79   *Seventy-nine*

G.C.   *TWA five three eight* climb and maintain flight level two four zero

G.C.   *National seventy-nine* climb and maintain twelve thousand

NAT79   *National seventy-nine* to twelve thousand

Listening to tapes of controller-pilot talk for some time, you pick up fragments of talk with other controllers sitting nearby, yawns, bits of song, gossip and sometimes normal flashes of annoyance quite beyond the strict code of FAA behavior, such as this comment from a Canadian Captain who figured he was just as alert as any controller.

G.C.   [*excited*] *Canada four nine,* you have traffic at twelve o'clock sharp at two miles southwest bound above you.

CAN49   [*sarcastic*] We have them in sight, father!

G.C.   Yahhhhhhhhhhhhh

Private
Planes

All planes except those operated by the commerical airlines come under the heading *general aviation*. This includes the small single engine planes people use for fun or business, the good-sized multijets owned by corporations to fly their executives and employees from plant to plant, police and forest-fire-fighting planes, air taxis, amulance planes, trainers, and helicopters used for almost everything. In other words, general aviation includes nearly all types of aircraft.

Because airports and control facilities get so much money from the Federal Government, many people, especially small plane owners, feel that any aircraft can use any airport in the country for takeoff or landing, and in fact this is perfectly legal. This can, and on occasion does, mean that a small single-engine prop plane lines up in the middle of a string of commercial jets on a busy airport runway, waiting its turn to take off. Or it can get itself into an approach sequence and come in for a landing during the evening rush hour. A very few airports have special runways for private planes, but if a pilot requests a full-length runway, controllers are required by law to give it to him. After all, he is a taxpayer and so is part owner of the facilities he is using.

However, many people do not think this is right or safe and believe small private planes should have their own airports, and they keep trying to pass laws to prevent private planes from using commercial runways. Small planes make big jetliner pilots nervous, even though some of them own and fly small planes of their own. Their slower speeds and smaller size make private planes harder to avoid. Some very small planes, particularly those with fabric wings, hardly show up at all on a controller's scope and can easily be overlooked when it is crowded with commercial planes. As a result, neither the small planes nor the big ones get the proper protection from controllers. Very small private planes seldom reach an altitude at which they tangle with commercial craft, except near airports, and here there have been bad accidents.

For instance, on a commercial flight not long ago, the pilot suddenly turned sharply to the left and dove almost straight down, throwing passengers in a heap. After people had sorted themselves out and the plane was again flying on a level course, the captain appeared in the cabin and said, "I want to apologize, ladies and gentlemen. That was just another taxpayer!"

A small plane, too light to produce a radar image, had crossed right in front of a big jet, and only sudden and violent action had saved all their lives. Since no controller could see the small plane on his scope, he could offer no help.

Private plane owners vigorously deny they are a danger to the big jets and accuse the airlines of a "powerful propaganda campaign" to discredit them in order to make bigger profits. Private pilots also point out that small planes help regular airline passengers by taking them all the way to their homes and offices, just as cars or buses or taxis do. After all, the big jets only fly between good-sized cities, and airports are often miles from where you want to go.

There are now about 116,000 general aviation aircraft in our skies, and about 2,700 commercial planes, nearly all jets, with more planes of both types appearing every day. Also there are usually around 20,000 military planes, which are also under the care of the FAA controllers.

Landing fees at airports, figured on the weight of the plane fully loaded, vary considerably from one part of the country to another, but very often a small, single-engine prop plane will pay about $5 to land, except during the evening rush hours between 3 and 8 PM. Then the fee usually goes up to as much as $25. This is done to discourage small planes from using a big airport at these times, but it doesn't always work. To men on urgent business, this extra money means nothing. Big commercial jets pay from around $80 to $104 to land at a major airport—less in smaller cities. Rates for the big new superjets have not yet been set.

Generally speaking there are two kinds of FAA flight rules —the IFR or Instrument Flight Rules used by commerical aircraft equipped with a full set of instruments, and the VFR or Visual Flight Rules used by most of the private planes and occasionally by commerical aircraft.

To fly IFR a plane must carry a good deal of very expensive electronic navigating equipment, and as a rule only the big airlines and the jets owned by big companies and a few wealthy individuals can afford these instruments.

Flying VFR is pretty much like driving a car. The pilot uses his eyes to watch out for other aircraft and trusts that other pilots will do the same. But this old idea that if you could "see and be seen" you were safe is no longer valid, for the skies are full of commercial—and sometimes private—jets which can fly at 600 mph, and by the time two planes flying at this speed see each other, it's too late. This is why we have radar and air controllers.

While commercial prop planes fly VFR on occasion, all

such planes are required to carry the equipment they need to fly IFR (Instrument Flight Rules). However, most general aviation planes—about 95,000—are single-engine craft and carry very limited equipment. Only the executive jets owned by corporations usually have a full set of electronic instruments. Commercial jets cannot fly VFR.

If a private pilot is flying VFR by day at some distance from an airport, FAA regulations require only that he carry an airspeed indicator, an altimeter, a compass and a few other elementary items. But if he goes near an airport he must not only be flying IFR but also have a two-way radio and several additional items. So far as controllers are concerned, the two-way radio is crucial. Without this the controller can do nothing to help a private pilot—nor can this man, when in need of information, talk to a controller.

If a private pilot flies above 24,000 feet—and while most seldom go above 10,000 feet, some new models can reach 24,000 feet—he should carry still more instruments for safety.

Something private pilots find invaluable are FAA's Flight Service Stations, of which there are over 330 scattered all over the United States. These Stations do not have radar or controllers, but by radio and land phones and a national teletype network they keep track of private planes, furnish them with weather reports, with special attention to winds, and accept their flight plans. Also, they help pilots who have lost their way, sometimes by the use of special strobe lights, which indicate the direction from which a call is coming. They also advise pilots who have mechanical trouble or become ill.

These Flight Service Stations, manned by from half a dozen men to sixty (in Washington, D.C.) are usually located in airports, for the convenience of pilots who wish to file flight plans.

Suppose a man is planning a flight from Chicago to Los Angeles. He may appear in person with a written VFR flight plan, or he may dictate it over the phone. In any event, the Chicago Station has his name, a description of his plane, his projected route, his destination, and the time he expects to arrive.

If this pilot does not show up after a reasonable time, overdue procedures are set in motion. First, the airports along his route are checked. Sometimes private pilots will stop along the way and park their planes in a hangar over-night—but fail to notify the Flight Service people. So air-ports along the way are asked to look in their hangars and ask about for such a plane. Using teletype, this can be done in a short time. Then, if no trace of this pilot or his plane is turned up, the Air-Sea Rescue Service is called on.

Private pilots with larger planes sometimes fly great dis-tances, even to Europe on occasion, taking the Great Circle Route, which allows for several refueling stops, and many are extraordinarily expert. But among the 116,000, more or less, who have their own planes, there are of course many who are novices and need a little help. In addition to the Flight Service Stations, there are of course the controllers all over the country, and private pilots are advised to turn to them for advice when they can reach them. Then it is up to a patient controller to quiet-talk an unlucky fellow down to a safe landing without either of them losing his cool.

With a skyful of jets due to land in a few minutes, this really puts a controller over the jumps. Almost every con-troller has a story of how he helped such a pilot. Talking to a flyer one evening, a controller in the New York Center soon realized that this pilot was not only lost but not very sure about the mechanics of his plane. So switching to a different radio frequency (not to embarrass the troubled pilot) he had a little talk with the pilot of an airline plane flying in the same direction, asking him to lead the small plane to the nearest airport. At the same time he urged him to take things easy "because this guy's kinda jumpy, and has problems. . . ."

Things worked out all right, and the controller was astonished some days later when the single-engine plane's pilot appeared at the radar room where he was on duty and thanked him profusely for saving his life! He'd discovered from the airline pilot what had happened.

In aviation nearly all estimates of future growth have proved to be short, but even taking these underestimates into account here's what the experts say things will look like in 1977. They say we'll have:

$$
\begin{array}{r}
3{,}500 \text{ commercial passenger jets} \\
180{,}000 \text{ general aviation planes} \\
\underline{20{,}000} \text{ military planes} \\
203{,}500 \text{ aircraft in our skies}
\end{array}
$$

As always, the busiest airspace in the United States will be in the "golden triangle"—the area between New York, Washington and Chicago.

Navaids

An odd thing about some of the dozens of navigation charts issued by the FAA for the pilots of both commercial and private planes is that they have almost none of the markings you see on ordinary maps. There are few cities or towns and no roads or railroads or rivers or state or county division—just airports and what pilots know as "navaids" or aids to aerial navigation. Sometimes a coastline is indicated very faintly and the names of towns are printed in small type near the VOR stations that help pilots navigate across country. On these charts the VOR stations look a little like clock faces, but have 360 degrees radiating from them instead of indicating hours and minutes.

The VOR (Visual Omni-Range) stations are located in very unimpressive little "towers" about twenty feet high set on small, one-story buildings in fields and open spaces all over the U.S. Each of the 360 signals broadcast by each of these stations goes out in a different direction, and each one is distinctive, so that a pilot tuned in on it knows in which direction he is going. The VOR stations usually operate automatically and have diesel-powered generators to take over if the local electric supply fails.

Commercial pilots, who must file a formal flight plan with the FAA before starting on a flight, usually go from one VOR station to another, picking one of the 360 signals which will take them in the right direction. Private planes also make use of the VOR stations. Over an extended flight this moving from one VOR to another may not be the shortest route in miles, but by selecting the right VOR stations a pilot can take into account the storms and high winds he wants to avoid to give his passengers the most comfortable ride.

And if a storm shifts after a plane has taken off, one of the enroute controllers will inform the pilot, and he may get permission to change his original flight plan.

In addition to the big navigation charts already mentioned, the FAA also has many other smaller maps it issues for airmen, such as its Local Aeronautical Charts, very popular with the pilots of smaller planes. These show a great many ground features such as towns, cities, roads, railroads, rivers, canals, big public buildings, and factories. Private pilots flying under 10,000 feet find such maps very useful.

Also of help to pilots are the omnitrack receivers on planes. When set on a distant transmitter, the pilot reads in a window, in a little black box, a series of changing numbers —"To . . . . . . miles." And after this point has been passed, the window in this little box will read "From . . . . . . miles."

However, a company's fast private jet usually flies "point to point," which means it flies in a straight line from one airport to another. While controllers monitor these flights, their pilots do not have to fly from one VOR to another and often make much better time. Business men in a hurry speed things by resorting to still another dodge. They avoid big airports such as Kennedy or O'Hare or L.A. International, where they may have to spend an hour or two waiting to

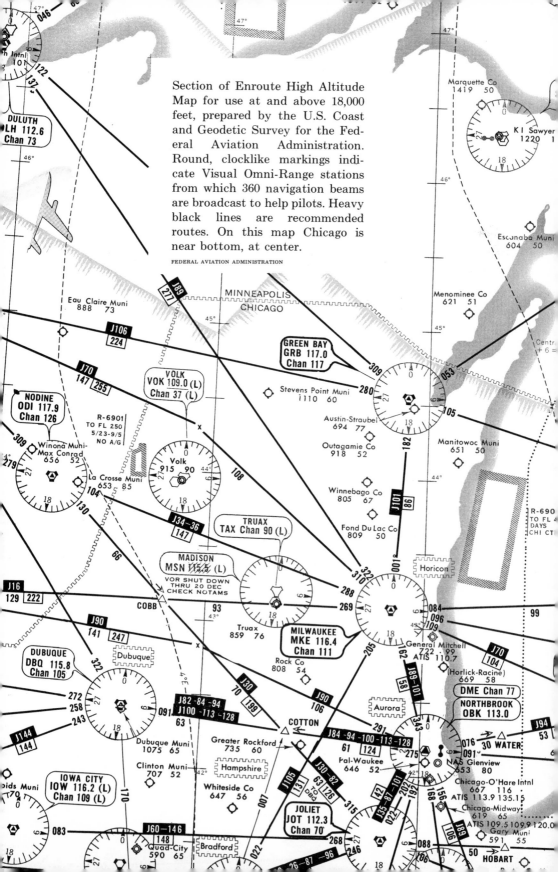

Section of Enroute High Altitude Map for use at and above 18,000 feet, prepared by the U.S. Coast and Geodetic Survey for the Federal Aviation Administration. Round, clocklike markings indicate Visual Omni-Range stations from which 360 navigation beams are broadcast to help pilots. Heavy black lines are recommended routes. On this map Chicago is near bottom, at center.

FEDERAL AVIATION ADMINISTRATION

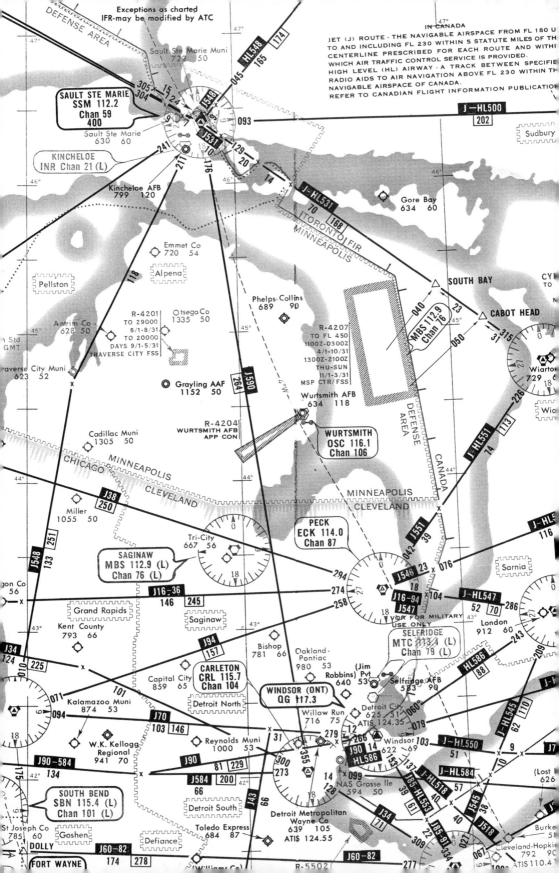

land. They have the company pilot drop them off at some small, little-used airport near the city. With no waiting in a holding pattern, and no traffic jams to fight at the airport, they may beat a competitor who has taken a commercial plane and is snarled in a road traffic tieup, even if the small airport they use is several miles from the city.

The bigger flight information maps, which measure about $3\frac{1}{4}$ by $1\frac{1}{2}$ feet, come in two kinds, Enroute Low Altitude Maps, which are for pilots flying up to about 18,000 feet, and High Altitude Maps for those flying above this. In the case of the Supersonic Transport, this will mean from 18,000 to maybe 65,000 feet. These maps are crammed with information which is constantly being checked by both pilots and the FAA, and many maps are reprinted every few months. Every pilot carries a full set of these maps in his giant briefcase—sometimes called his "brainbag." All of these maps are made for the FAA by the Coast and Geodetic Survey in Washington.

On High Altitude Maps covering a part of the eastern seaboard of the United States appear a series of very large blocks of airspace which are reserved by the military for training and for the testing of bombs, rockets and other weapons. These extend from Maine to Miami. While some of these areas are only infrequently in use, pilots cannot fly into them without special permission. However, some areas, such as the airspace just east of Norfolk, Virginia, are used about half of the time. The result of these restrictions is that planes to or from Europe must use a few comparatively small channels of free airspace—and there are no holding patterns over the ocean, even in the congested New York area.

There are also many areas all over the United States used for weapons testing which are restricted and therefore marked on the FAA maps, and near military installations there are narrow, triangular, spaces that can be used for the takeoff of military aircraft and must be kept clear of any nonmilitary planes.

Will New Inventions Replace Controllers?

Although a controller's job is now pretty well defined, his equipment is changing all the time and will probably continue to change a great deal more in the future. Because a controller is so vital to safe and smooth flying and is often under terrific nervous tension, electronics engineers and the FAA have been working for years to find ways of automating his work and making it a little simpler. The idea is to relieve the controller of some of the small housekeeping chores that distract him and force him to take his eyes from the scope. For instance, there is the business of writing on the shrimp boats and then pushing them across the face of the scope as the planes move—and the need to write additional notations on the Flight Progress Strips from time to time.

While there are four different types of controllers working at each radarscope, the radar controller, also known as a "Journeyman Controller," is the boss and makes all the decisions. He is assisted by a "coordinator," who accepts and gives handoffs of planes entering or leaving this Sector's airspace—also a very responsible job. Then there are the "D" man, who puts the shrimp boats in place and does other chores, and the assistant controller. But it is the radar controller who advises the pilots high in the sky and watches their planes on his scope. In a way, he has both his ears and his eyes on echos of these distant, invisible planes. His life is devoted to keeping them safely separated.

Consequently, when he has to work six days a week, and on occasion ten hours a day, this is bad for everybody— the passengers, the pilots, their planes—and the controller. A nervous, exhausted controller is bound to make poor judgments. Many controllers recall evenings when their only supper was a cup of coffee, brought to them at their stations, which grew cold before they could get to it. So anything that can relieve the strain will be welcomed.

Antennas of the Los Angeles Center at Palmdale, Calif. They relay radar signals from the Center's distant rotating antennas down to the radarscopes.

LOS ANGELES DEPT. OF AIRPORTS

Certainly pilots appreciate the overtime pay they earn for anything above their standard forty-hour week, but the $20,000 a year a few top men earn for a 55-hour to 60-hour week doesn't make up for the strain. Controllers complain they never see their families and seldom have any time off and would rather earn less and lead more normal lives. A great deal of the time there seem to be far too few competent, well-trained controllers.

Controllers seldom talk about it, but they can never forget that thousands of feet above them in the sky each of them is guiding perhaps a dozen planes each with a hundred or more people who are eating, sleeping, talking, reading—all with a complete faith in the pilot and his unseen, even unknown, associates the radar controllers.

A plane coming down through a fog or darkness relies on a few brief exchanges of words with an airport's controllers such as "*Eastern 565* come down to 4500 [feet]—*TWA 362* turn right—cut to 300 [mph]—*Pan Am 442* descend to 2500 —OK, you're set for a final approach." Talking a plane into an approach lineup so that it will always be the required three to five miles behind the plane ahead of it, and still not crowd the plane following it, requires every bit of a controller's experience and attention. On a radarscope planes heading for a landing, although still hundreds or even thousands of feet in the air, show up as an amazingly straight column of pairs of blips. Soon the passengers in the PAN AM 442 hear the preliminary "thump" as the wheels go down, and then that other small, reassuring bump as the wheels first touch the runway, and finally the roar of the jets as the pilot uses their reverse thrust to help bring the plane to a stop.

For about thirty years a controller's basic equipment has been a radarscope, which shows where every plane is located in the Sector he is watching. Following the movement of aircraft across his scope, he controls traffic by first identifying the blips on his scope with a squawk-ident, and then talking to pilots and tagging their planes' blips with little plastic

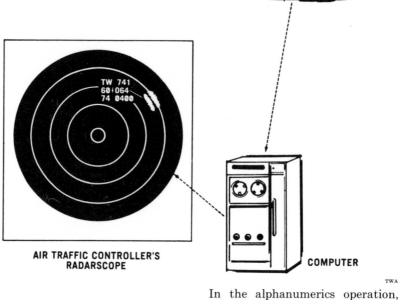

**AIR TRAFFIC CONTROLLER'S
RADARSCOPE**

COMPUTER

TWA

In the alphanumerics operation,
signals from the plane's altimeter
are sent into a computer, which
controls the changing altitude
figures the controller sees on his
scope.

shrimp boats, or by watching the alphanumerics tags that
identify them. This has become a standard procedure in all
Centers and airports in the United States with very few
exceptions.

Under light traffic conditions, when a controller has but
five or six planes on his scope—say around 10 AM—the
shrimp-boat system works well enough. But air travel is a
booming business, and already the airspace around major
airports gets dangerously crowded during the rush hours.
There are rush hours at airports just as there are rush
hours in the subway. Between 7 and 9 AM, and 5 and 8 in
the evening, controllers are under terrific pressure. This is
the time most business men are flying, and the evening is

the time when it is often necessary to send large numbers of planes into holding patterns. Except for the summer vacation period, about half of all flying is for business reasons, and a great number of the men who take such trips try to get home early in the evening.

Forseeing an enormous growth in air traffic back in the 1950s, designers started working to help controllers, and in the late 1950s they came up with the fantastic system called *alphanumerics,* another way of saying "letters and numbers." This uses "responsive" or cooperating instruments in a plane's cockpit, as well as a computer located in the control building.

(One of the problems here, of course, is that not all planes carry the same equipment, some of which is very expensive, even though about ninety percent of all airliners are made in the United States. Different airlines have different ideas.)

The first version of alphanumerics was tested in the Indianapolis Center in 1965-1966. This involved a change in the radarscope itself. Important bits of information from the plane and other data from a computer are shown electronically right on the face of the radarscope, next to the blips of the plane they represent. This information, including the abbreviation for the name of the airline, the number of the flight, and the plane's altitude, appears in a neat little block of numbers and letters written in glowing light, called a tag. There are three parts to the alphanumerics system: the computer, the radarscope and the digitizer, which turns the data the controller needs into the figures on the scope.

Most important of all, alphanumerics shows the plane's exact altitude every second. This figure is transmitted automatically from an altimeter on the plane, changing constantly as the plane flies up or down. New altitude figures appear every hundred feet. Assuming for example, that a plane is at 5,300 feet and is coming down for a landing, the controller would read on its alphanumerics tag 530—520—510—500—490, and so forth. In many operations controllers and computers drop off the final zero to save time and space. Actually these figures mean 5,300, 5,200, 5,100, 5,000 and 4,900 feet.

These little tags stick close to the blips of the planes they belong to so as not to get mixed up, almost like people in a crowd, moving out of each others' way.

Controllers say this "instant altitude" is about the most important improvement they have had yet. With the shrimp boat system they have to ask a pilot what his altitude is and then tell him what altitude he should go to next. And after they have told him to move up or down, they don't know just when he has followed their instructions or how far he has gone. One of the chief limitations of the present radar is that it does not show a plane's altitude. Controllers say that the alphanumerics system gives them what they call "three-dimensional radar."

This column of letters and numbers on a controller's scope has been stored there by the computer to await the arrival of the planes these tags represent. About 15 minutes before one of these planes is due to land and its blips are on the scope, the proper tag will slide across the scope and attach itself to these blips.

CREIGHTON PEET

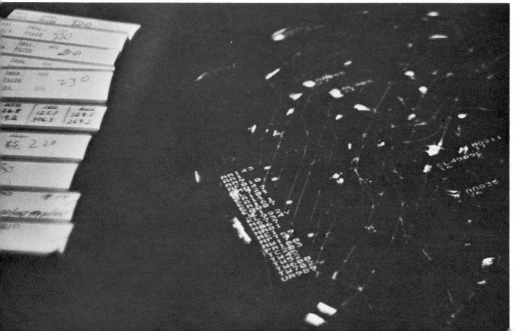

With the conventional radar a controller doesn't know whether a plane he is following is at 4,000 or 10,000 feet. He knows about how far away it is, and how far from another plane it is—or seems to be. So if a controller sees two sets of blips getting too close he tells one or both planes to change course, although one plane might be at 10,000 feet and the other at 15,000, so that there was no possibility of a collision. He only knows this after checking with both pilots. But with alphanumerics a controller knows instantly the altitude of each plane. This information comes to him automatically.

Neither the pilot nor the controller has to do anything to produce these altitude figures, which are transmitted from the plane in response to an interrogation from the controller's alphanumerics system.

Some of the information that appears on the scope day after day is what the controllers call the "canned program." It is fairly standard and is fed into the radarscopes every day from the computer, where it is stored. Its origin is quite separate from the alphanumerics tags.

These "canned programs" are much like the timetables used by airline passengers. For example, every day at certain hours there will be flights arriving from Chicago, Atlanta, New York, Paris and Tokyo, and others leaving for London, Milwaukee, and Memphis. This information is of course known weeks in advance. So, early each morning, the computer prints out on Flight Progress Strips the basic information on the planes due in the next few hours. Then an assistant controller snaps these strips into little plastic holders, which look something like the racks in which Scrabble players keep their letters.

These slips and their holders are then stored in the racks above the proper radarscope. When one of these planes appears on his scope and he has identified it, the controller reaches up and takes its strip down and puts it with those of the other planes he is watching. Sometime before this, maybe half an hour, the computer has transmitted to the radarscope a list of perhaps a dozen flights due in this time span. That column of figures and letters appears at one side of the scope, until the blips of one of the expected planes appears. Then the alphanumerics tag for this plane slides across the scope and attaches itself to the proper blips. At about the same time the controller gets a handoff of this same plane from another man, and it is now his responsibility.

What the controller has to watch for are delays, changes in routing, bad weather and special situations. And of course, most important of all, the controller advises the pilots when to change altitude, speed, and direction, and he watches constantly to make sure they have the proper separation.

Engineers say that in the future their alphanumerics systems will do a great deal more. A one-time pilot, a controller for the past ten years, believes that one day when a controller presents a computer with a list of possibly ten planes due to arrive in the next half hour, the computer will be programmed to select the order in which those planes should be brought down. The plan would not have anything to do with the actual location of these planes, or their nearness to the airport. The computer, knowing the flight characteristics and capabilities of each make of aircraft would give the controller a list showing the order in which the planes should be landed, and he would then inform their captains.

Computers programmed to know the characteristics and capabilities of every model and every make of plane would never recommend that a plane do anything of which it was not capable. If a controller gave an order that was not right for a particular plane, the computer would immediately tell him he was wrong. Some planes require more room to make a turn than others. In a tight situation such planes should not be forced to fly too close to other planes.

You might wonder if in a few years planes will fly without pilots or controllers to guide them, but the more complicated a piece of equipment gets, the more difficult it is to adjust when something goes wrong. Today most planes carry two different navigating systems and use both of them to figure their positions, checking one result against the other. TWA's 747 jumbo jets carry *three* sets of inertial navigating equipment to make sure that one will always be working properly. Flying is not a business to fool around with, and airlines and pilots are glad to have aboard as much equipment as possible to insure their safety. No matter how smart machines get, passengers will always feel safer when real live pilots rather than autopilots are up front in the cockpit, and real live controllers, rather than blinking computers, are watching radarscopes down on the ground.

Actually, nobody has ever thought planes could do without controllers, no matter how efficient the computers and alphanumerics systems become. Always there comes the situation in which human judgment is essential, and a controller can solve a difficult problem and save a plane from disaster by ordering maneuvers not programmed into the computer. Even if both shrimp boats and Flight Progress Strips are eliminated, controllers will be essential.

The biggest problem in aircraft control is the fantastic speed with which aviation is developing everywhere. Jets and airports and crowds of passengers get bigger every year, and none of the plans made two or three years before continue to hold up. All over America, passenger trains are being discontinued and stations are turned into stores, offices and homes. Big ocean liners are being scrapped or turned into resort hotels or night clubs. People who once rode on these trains and ships are crowding into airports and planes.

Chiefly, controllers are concerned about two things: airspace and "concrete"—by which they mean runways in airports. They say they haven't enough of either. They think the airspace problem can be solved without too much trouble if we can get more up-to-date control devices that will allow us to fly planes closer together with safety. Already there is a strong movement to reduce the horizontal separation of planes flying the Atlantic air lanes from 120 miles to 60 miles. An improved alphanumerics system might make it possible to crowd more planes into the airspace above our airports than we have now.

In 1968 still another effort was made to get more use from our existing airspace. A new Common IFR Room was set up at Kennedy Airport in New York, where all the radar control equipment of three of the country's largest airports—Kennedy, LaGuardia, and Newark (N.J.), all in the New York area—was consolidated in a single room.

Each airport still has its own separate radarscopes and controllers, but all of these men and all of this equipment are only a few feet away from each other. In the past each of the airports was surrounded by a buffer zone to prevent accidents, a ring of airspace no planes were supposed to penetrate. The new idea is that the buffer zones and even, at times, sections of any airport's airspace may be used by planes from a different airport for a brief period—maybe a minute or two.

This is something like using the opposing lane of a motor highway when you can see it is clear of traffic—which can be a pretty risky thing down on the ground. But radar controllers can see much farther than motorists and be sure the airspace they are borrowing is safe to use. Before they do this, however, they ask one of the other airport's controllers for the loan of this airspace. Usually the other man is sitting only a few feet away in their Common IFR Room, so contact with him is instantaneous. There's no getting him on the phone and waiting till he's checked the situation over.

The Common IFR Room at Kennedy, where controllers move about over a soft carpet, is like no other radar room anywhere. There's a great deal of conversation between both the arrival and departure controllers of these three large airports. The men frequently stand up and walk about to consult with other controllers a few feet away; all are monitoring aircraft in the same 3,000 square miles of airspace, and controlling sometimes seems to be a community effort. The only controllers left at the LaGuardia and Newark airports are the takeoff men in the tower cabs, using their eyes and binoculars to follow aircraft.

The temporary borrowing of a nearby airport's airspace can relieve traffic congestion and speed things along generally. Airports are always in need of more and more airspace. In theory a single large airport should handle a maximum of sixty operations (takeoffs and landings) per hour, but on August 7, 1968, Kennedy airport alone handled 138 flights in one hour. Combining control of Kennedy, LaGuardia and Newark makes this kind of crowding less dangerous. Altogether, these three airports handle over 1,235,000 plane movements a year, in which about thirty-seven million passengers are involved.

As speeds increase, controllers get nervous about putting more and more planes in a limited airspace. The big SSTs (supersonic transports) of the future will increase the speed of the "rate of closure" from the present 1,200 mph to 3,600 mph. This means that today two planes each going at 600 mph will have a 1,200 mph rate of closure, which is the speed at which they could come together and crash if not properly separated. But two SSTs, each flying at 1,800 mph, could come together at the rate of 3,600 mph. Preventing a disastrous accident will present new problems.

As one controller remarked, "If one SST was leaving the New York area and another was approaching it and we turned one of them aside, he might be right in the middle of the Boston traffic before we could do anything about it. (Normal flying time to Boston from New York is about forty-five minutes). And then this controller added, "This speed is too fast for human minds to project." Present plans are not only to keep the SSTs from flying over inhabited land but also to cut their speed when making an approach to an airport so that they will be flying at the same speed as average planes.

As for the problem of "concrete," which would mean more runways, so that more planes could take off and be landed at the same time—this sometimes seems impossible. In many cities real estate men have been allowed to sell building lots so close to the existing airport runways that it is impossible to build new ones.

These lots covered with houses that are filled with people have brought other problems. Naturally the people complain about the noise of the jets in their back yards. Lawyers and politicians join in complaining that the airport is a public nuisance. In some cases (as at Kennedy in New York, for instance) nearby homeowners have succeeded in forcing the airport to close one of the main runways for long periods of time. Also, pilots are supposed to cut their power just as they are taking off, to reduce the noise, a procedure they consider very dangerous, and they often ignore this rule when they have a heavy load.

Real estate men planning the sale of land or houses near an airport have approached controllers, promising to make it worth their while if they would keep all planes away from a certain area at a certain time while their prospects were inspecting the property. The controllers in question were naturally outraged, and the suggestion was preposterous. The routes taken by planes arriving or departing from an airport cannot be changed on a whim.

Although pilots, controllers and FAA officials all agree that the equipment controllers are now using should be replaced with more modern devices, this is not an easy matter. Air control is an extremely complicated business, and nobody is absolutely sure which systems will be best. Such firms as IBM and Raytheon have worked on the problem, and models of new devices are continually being tested in the FAA laboratories in Atlantic City, but engineers are always promising more and still more improvements. One of the early models of the alphanumerics setup was tried out for a year at the New York Center, but it was removed when irritated controllers took to turning it off. Since then that system has been greatly improved and is now in use in the IFR Room at Kennedy Airport and in Atlanta. FAA executives complain that with new ideas coming up every few months it is very hard to know which equipment to buy.

But no matter how many improvements are made, there will be always the problem of fitting human beings into a computer setup almost as a part of the computer. Finding even ordinarily competent controllers is not easy; finding superhuman ones may be impossible.

Much of the radar equipment now in use in airports and Centers is similar to that in use twenty years ago. Controllers are continually complaining through their unions, particularly PATCO (Professional Air Traffic Controllers Organization), that it should be replaced with more modern equipment. But paying the millions—or possible billions— of dollars needed to replace all of our air control equipment is more complicated. Up to now, all of the Centers and radar control rooms in airports have been paid for and operated by the Federal Government, under the Department of Transportation.

But with a war, trips to the moon and poverty programs to pay for, Congress thinks of air control in terms of comparatively small sums of money each year. At the present rate it would take about twenty years to update all the equipment controllers use. Many would still be shoving shrimp boats around in 1990! As for the many small airports that currently have no radarscope to watch their takeoffs and landings, they don't figure much in the plans, although they are growing at a terrific rate.

Recently it has been proposed that airline passengers be taxed to provide the needed money for new control equipment. It has also been suggested that air freight, the airlines themselves, and aviation gasoline be taxed to raise needed money.

Another thing bothering controllers is that there never seem to be enough of them. They say that some of those given FAA certificates are not capable of handling really complex situations. During a period in the 1960s no new controllers at all were turned out by the Federal Aviation

Academy in Oklahoma City, which was closed at the time, because the Federal Government was having an "austerity program." That loss of manpower is only slowly being made up.

Still another important consideration in planning and installing new control and navigation equipment is the fact that practically all big airlines fly all over the world. Air France flies in Mexico and the United States, Japan Airlines flies in the United States and England, and TWA, BOAC and others fly practically around the world. New control systems to guide planes must have responsive equipment aboard the planes of these airlines. A piece of equipment may cost well over $100,000, and many airlines are reluctant to equip a big fleet of planes with a device that may well be outdated in a few years.

Even in the Continental United States there is absolutely no such thing as standard, identical equipment on every plane flying overhead. Different aircraft builders and different airlines all have their own ideas. The FAA has certain rules about basic equipment which of course everybody obeys, but some of the new gadgets are very fancy and very expensive, even if they are as good as their inventors say they are.

How Radar Works

Radar, the device that gives controllers their vital eye on the sky, not only sees through the darkest night but also cuts through fog and reaches a distance of about 150 miles in all directions. Since radar beams go in a straight line like TV signals, they do not bend around the curvature of the earth. The higher the radar antenna, the farther the beams will go and the larger the area a radar covers. A plane's radar can reach hundreds of miles, if it is high enough. A heavy rain or snow storm makes the picture on a radar-scope blank out temporarily.

Sitting in front of his scope, a controller can instantly change the size of the area he is watching by simply turning a switch. That is, he can, in effect, "blow up" his picture so that everything he sees is in a small circle five miles in diameter. Or he can switch over to a scale that covers per-haps a hundred miles in all directions. While he sees more this way, of course, he loses a great deal of detail.

RCA

How a radar works: From the radar's rotating antenna, signals fly up and bounce off a plane. Returning almost instantly, signals are channeled to a radar-scope where each plane appears as a pair of blips (slashes.) The shape of the plane has nothing to do with the shape of the blips.

Radar works by sending out electromagnetic beams, or pulses, which send back electronic echoes when they hit an object, or "target." The pulses travel at the speed of light— 186,000 miles a second—both going out and coming back. Despite the tremendous speed with which the pulses travel, there is an interval between one burst of pulses and the next, during which the transmitter is turned off. In that time the sending antenna becomes a receiver for the echo of the preceeding burst of pulses. But the whole process is so fast that in a single second thousands of pulses go out and send back echoes, all of which finally appear as a radar picture on the face of the controller's radarscope.

The radar transmitter-receiver, the dish-like framework you have seen on the tops of hills, buildings and ships, is constantly turning around to cover its area. Every time the

Splashes of light attached to a plane's blips are the fading remains of the plane's previous positions. (Remember, shape of the plane has nothing to do with shape of blips.) In the center of this picture Trans World flight 125 is moving straight to the *left,* leaving a blur of light to the right of its blips.

CREIGHTON PEET

radar antenna's sharply focused beam hits a "target," it produces a picture of it on the scope.

These echoes on the face of the radarscope don't last long. They start to fade immediately. However, the next time the transmitter-receiver dish turns around, it reinforces these fading echoes on the scope with new ones, making them bright and light again. This happens about every three to four seconds.

But of course if the targets—in the controller's case the planes moving across his scope—have moved, the new echoes will be in slightly different locations on the scope. This is what the controller is watching—the changing locations of his planes.

On the pictures of radarscopes in this book you will notice that the planes' blips are often blurred, seldom sharp and clear. This is because there are always faint trails of light left from the plane's previous positions, something like the foaming wake of a ship passing through water. They are very useful to controllers. They are a positive indication of the direction in which the plane is moving.

Radar is not only very versatile but also very complicated, and it is used to do all kinds of jobs. There is a kind of radar in nature. Bats use their own "radar" to keep from hitting each other and the walls of the dark caves they live in. A bat sends out a supersonic tone with his vocal organs with a range far beyond anything human beings can hear. A bat's notes range from 30,000 to 70,000 vibrations a second, and their ears are tuned to receive echoes from such sounds as they fly about their caves. Scientists have tested bats by stringing wires in totally dark rooms—but the bats never ran into them.

Moonlighting
in
the
Moonlight

After 12 PM most passenger flights come to an end. People don't want to stay up later than this, and usually they don't need to, because you can fly anywhere in the United States by daylight.

But big jetliners cost millions of dollars, and more and more airlines are making them work all night as well as all day to earn their keep.

As soon as the last passengers have left, certain planes (known as "QC" or quick change) planes, are put into service as cargo carriers, moving tons of freight from one city to another while most of us are asleep in bed. They are, in fact, "moonlighting" in a real sense—working at an extra job after hours.

Flying with them are the fleets of all-cargo planes, also moving by night, which most of us seldom see. These planes look like regular airships but have no windows at all along their sides.

First step in preparing a QC plane for its cargo-carrying job is to roll up a monstrous structure called a seat van.

Next, all the seats, which are mounted on movable pallets, are rolled out and stored in the seat van.

It takes only half an hour to remove not only all the plane's seats but also the galleys where the food is prepared.

When the regular planes leave the passenger apron of an airport, they taxi to the freight-loading area, where they are completely transformed in thirty minutes and loaded in another half hour.

First the workmen bring up an enormous structure on wheels, called a seat van, which looks like a small building. A very large door is opened in the plane, and the seat van is moved up and fastened to it. Then all the seats in the plane are rolled out into the van. This is very easy. One man can move six seats at once just by pushing them. The seats are fastened to "pallets" or thin platforms, which can be unlocked, and the steel floor of the plane cabin is covered with castors, or little rollers. When the pallets are unlocked, the seats all roll into the seat van one right after another, and soon the cabin is just a big empty tunnel.

Even the stewardesses' food-service galley, the tiny kitchen where they fix passengers' meals, is mounted on a pallet, and it also is rolled out into the van. Some vans are heated in winter and cooled in summer. While the plane is back up in the air carrying cargo, cleaners and inspectors are going over all the seats and galley, getting everything in shape for the first early-morning flight, around 6 AM, by which time all of the seats will have been rolled back in place.

Loading cargo into or out of one of the planes is a fast job, because everything is neatly packed long ahead of time in enormous fiberglass "igloos" shaped to fit exactly into the interior shell of the plane. An average passenger plane takes eight of these igloos, each holding 390 cubic feet of freight.

For controllers, the 11 PM to 7 AM shift—even with the air filled with cargo-carrying planes—is a time for relaxation. Night traffic is usually only about twenty percent of daytime traffic, even though air cargo is increasing constantly. Some airlines have economy flights after midnight, and a few passengers usually show up for special mail flights, which take off around midnight for distant cities with their first class sections piled high with mail bags, and some trans-

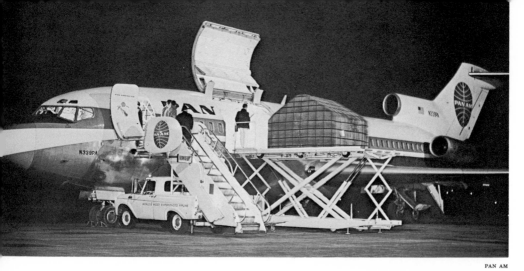

Cargo, neatly packed in "igloos" long ahead of time, fits neatly into the empty cabin space, and in another half hour the plane is on its way.

pacific flights carry half passengers and half cargo, a little like an old-time railroad day coach. Usually there are only three people aboard one of the QC planes—the pilot, the co-pilot and the engineer—making such a flight a dark and lonely business, with only street lights outlining the cities and only the cargo areas of airports humming with activity.

Some QC planes work their schedules so that they always return to the airport where they left their seats; others, such as those which make the New York-Chicago-Los Angeles jump in the dark, pick up a different but identical set of seats left in L.A. by an eastbound plane. Not all planes, by any means, have the capacity to convert to cargo carriers. United Airlines, which has about 387 planes, has only 36 QCs, as well as a big fleet of straight cargo carriers.

While it is never possible to stop air surveillance of any Sector, it is often possible to combine several Sectors on one radarscope when traffic is very light, so that one controller can cover a much greater area. This is easily done by turning a switch on a radarscope so that it includes areas usually covered by two or three Sectors.

The early-morning hours are also used for training new

controllers, or for familiarizing men from another part of the country with the particular problems of a new area. In the long, comparatively quiet after-midnight sessions men can talk more freely and learn more of their exacting business than they could during the tensions of a rush hour.

But if the pace slackens between 1 and 6 AM, this is only temporary. By 7 AM the takeoff controllers up in the airport's cab can look out over their runways and see an endless line of planes waiting for them to give the word to become airborne.

The Airspace People

Aircraft controllers must be intelligent, imaginative, accurate, quick, aggressive, resourceful self-starters who stay calm in a crisis and have good memories and a flair for numbers. Also, and perhaps primarily, they must have what their instructors at the FAA Academy in Oklahoma City call a "three-dimensional capability." They must be able to think in terms of three dimensions.

When a controller first sits down in front of his scope to start work, he has to "build a matrix in his mind"—or as we say, he has to "get the picture." That is he must create for himself, in his mind, a three-dimensional picture of the airspace through which the planes on his scope are flying. It takes a few minutes to do this. A man settles into the situation after looking everything over carefully. Only then can he really take over from the previous controller on the job.

Many people, including engineers, architects and sculptors, must be able to think in three dimensions, but the things they deal with usually stay still. The aircraft controller's planes, which he sees only indirectly through the blips on his scope, are usually moving at terrific speeds. And they are moving through airspace, something most of us don't really understand.

A controller thinks of a section of airspace as a specific place, as specific as a corner of your living room. When he sends a BOAC flight into a holding pattern at, say, the 15,000 foot level, he remembers that he has a TWA flight at 14,000, and an Eastern Airlines at 13,000. And in his mind he sees circling not only these three planes but four other planes below them—at 12,000, 11,000, 10,000 and 9,000 feet—as distinctly as though they were layers in a gigantic cake.

At another time, when he directs a plane to make a turn to avoid collision with an unseen plane still many miles away, this situation is as real to him as though he were turning his car in the street in front of his house to avoid hitting a neighbor's car.

A number of planes lined up in an approach sequence at, say, 6-4,000 feet on their way to a landing, seem to a controller not too different from as many buses rumbling along over route 66, while the airspace under them is just as real to him as is the concrete highway under the buses.

And when a controller directs a pilot to take his plane to 21,000 feet, he thinks of this location as being just as real as the twenty-first floor of an office building. The fact that airspace has no road signs or landmarks is unimportant. All of us can talk about 30,000 feet or 40,000 feet, but for most of us it is just talk. For airspace people these are real places.

There are now about 9,000 full radar controllers in the United States, watching our skies through radarscopes twenty-four hours a day in three shifts. Also, there are about eleven thousand more assistant controllers and technicians, doing a wide variety of associated jobs. Most of these men are between the ages of twenty-two and thirty-five. The few in their forties usually have been moved to less critical posts.

Controlling is primarily a young man's job, because its nervous tensions are terrific. Some men have steel nerves and an amazing capacity to keep on making split-second decisions indefinitely, but most slow down, hesitate and show signs of uncertainty as they get older. Then the supervisors—and there is one for every ten controllers—watch them carefully. If they discover that a man is indeed slowing down, he is moved to a less tense position. Sometimes controllers remove themselves—through nervous breakdowns or hypertension. Many have ulcers, and an FAA survey discovered that four times as many controllers have coronary diseases as Air Force men of the same age.

On occasion a controller has simply left his job permanently, without explanations. One experienced controller put it this way: "It takes a man about five years to learn the business and earn his certification, and after four or five years more he's reached his peak and is at his best. Then, after another year or two, he starts to slow down; his responses, decisions and reactions take an extra second or two. By the time he's forty he's 'no longer right for the hot jobs.' "

Nearly all controllers are high school graduates, and many have had several years of college, but there are no educational requirements of any kind for this job. The only thing required is that a man must have had at least three years of "general experience," which might mean almost any kind of work. Many applicants for controllers' jobs have pilots' licenses or have worked as airline dispatchers, but academic work does not seem to be very important. This is probably the only work at which a man can earn between $13,000 and $20,000 a year without having had any specific educational background. While the FAA training required to become a controller takes from three to five years, not even a high school diploma is required to get a start. If a man likes the work and can do it, that's all that counts. Formal education will cut the number of years required to earn certification, but Ph.D.s have failed completely to pass the exams to become controllers.

For many years civilian controllers have come chiefly from the armed services—men who have served as controllers in the Army or Air Force—and the FAA gets lists of such men being discharged and offers them jobs in its Centers and airports. However, increasingly the FAA is taking care of all aircraft control in the United States, even where the armed forces are involved, so there are fewer men coming from the services.

Today controllers are being recruited by the U.S. Civil Service through posters in Post Offices and regional appeals in newspapers and on the radio and TV. Since there are no schools offering courses in radar controlling, except of course the FAA Academy in Oklahoma City, it is necessary to start from scratch, with men who think they might be interested in this work and can pass the preliminary exams. As a result, the FAA's Academy in Oklahoma City, where aircraft controllers take a nine-to-fourteen-week course to start them off, finds that from twenty to thirty percent of the men who first try out for this work have left before they have completed their three to five years of training to become full radar controllers.

The Federal Aviation Administration Academy at Oklahoma City, where controllers get their preliminary training, is housed in modern buildings equipped with a variety of specialized teaching machines and devices that simulate problems with which a controller might find himself confronted. Through earphones, the student listens to tapes of actual controller-pilot talk, and on practice radarscopes he follows simulated targets while instructors point out how each situation should be handled. The student also has a certain number of hours of regular classroom work each week. At each man's desk there are three buttons with which he can indicate his answers to the instructor's questions, but his choices show up only on the instructor's panel and are not seen by other students.

At present, student controllers learn to handle both the manual control system, using the little plastic shrimp boats, and the alphanumerics system, which is expected to be in use in all major Centers and airports in coming years.

As soon as he enters the Academy an applicant gets a rigid physical examination, with special attention to his eyesight (which is repeatedly tested every so often as long as he stays in this work). Then he takes an aptitude test that will discover, among other things, a man's capacity to visualize in three dimensions. Finally, after a short time he gets a special psychological test to discover any oddities of temperament that would make him unsuitable for this very special work. In this test examiners present the student with difficult and tricky situations in which a controller might find himself. Then they watch his performance and reactions to decide whether he would crack under stress or keep his cool. A controller's decisions are final. He has to be right the first time. He can't change his mind about planes flying at 600 miles an hour. Too many lives are involved.

Some controllers get their start at Centers or airports after doing clerical or assistant work around the radar rooms. Every facility has instructors and a few special radarscopes on which a man can pick up the beginnings of his craft. If he seems to have a feeling for the work and shows some ability, supervisors send him to the FAA Academy in Oklahoma City for the regular nine-to-fourteen-week intensive training course. With previous experience as a pilot or airline dispatcher, he may take one of the shorter courses. After he leaves the Oklahoma City school, most of a controller's training is on the job, sitting at a regular radarscope position with a full controller, either at a Center or an airport, watching and learning. At other times he takes regular classroom work. Finally, late at night when traffic is very light, he may spend time with controllers who have freedom to talk and make fuller explanations when they have very few planes on their scopes. This would be around 1 and 6 AM.

Obviously not all men who start in this work are really interested in it or capable of becoming controllers, and while

Classroom desks in the Oklahoma City school for controllers are equipped with many devices used by full controllers, but not radarscopes.

Still working without radarscopes, students learn manual control while listening through earphones to instructors in adjoining rooms, who are simulating pilots.

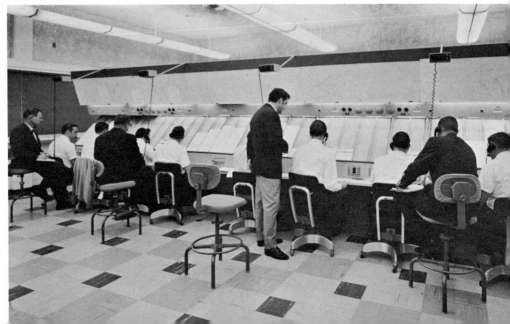

FEDERAL AVIATION AGENCY

In one three-week course students are drilled in basic procedures, how to align and adjust radar equipment, and how to read and interpret radarscope display.

Representatives from developing nations come to the Oklahoma School to learn the rudiments of the U.S. Air Traffic Control system.

FEDERAL AVIATION AGENCY

In the last six days of their training, students sit before standard radarscopes to put into use what they have learned. After leaving Oklahoma City they will spend 2-3 years watching and assisting full controllers in airports or Centers.

As part of his schooling a man works in the National Airspace System computer room, where he must develop and process a problem under an instructor's supervision.

Periodically supervisors and representative controllers from all over the country are called to Oklahoma City to take refresher courses and learn of new equipment. These 16 men are graduates of the first such class.

instructors try to warn all candidates by giving them a realistic picture of a controller's life at the start, many drop out after a year or two. The work is not only mentally exhausting but physically confining. Often a man is on duty in a darkened radar room eight or ten hours at a time, and his only physical exercise is to stand up and walk a few steps to speak to another controller. The radarscope in front of him never blinks or closes its lime-green eye—its eye on the sky.

Because so much depends on a controller's judgment and fast thinking, his performance is checked constantly. Every word he and a pilot exchange is automatically recorded on a tape, and the tapes are saved for several weeks. In case of an accident, or what some controllers refer to as a "deal situation," tapes are of course examined carefully and type-

scripts are made for hearings or trials. Also increasingly being watched are what pilots and controllers call "near
misses," when two planes come closer than they should
without actually touching. Not all of these are reported by
anybody, but there are enough to keep officials concerned.
Even if there has been no accident—only a near miss—a
controller may be brought up for a hearing by a committee,
which listens to tapes of his performance and questions him
closely. In 1967, 4,500 "hazardous near collisions" were reported.

All of this not only keeps a controller on his toes but often
makes him nervous. If one of the planes in his care has had
an accident, even though he was in no way to blame, or he
has seen a number of near misses on his scope, a controller
may simply quit and decide to make his living some other
way.

Controllers' pay has been increased in recent years and is
now very good. Training-on-the-job pay starts at $7,639 a
year and after one year goes to $9,320. A certified manual
controller gets $11,233, a limited radar man $13,389, and a
full radar man (after three and a half years) gets $15,812.
However, controllers in many places earn a great deal of
overtime, often working six days a week and ten-hour days.
Saturday, Sunday and holiday pay is twenty-five percent
higher than regular pay, and there is a ten percent increase
for night work. In a big airport, such as Kennedy, O'Hare
or Los Angeles International, several top controllers make
over $20,000 a year. Supervisors get around $23,000.

Looking at a roomful of controllers bent over their radarscopes in a big Center, you see no suggestion of the heroic,
and no evidence of the horrendous responsibilities these men
live with hour after hour, week after week. Just a lot of
youngish men all dressed in what amounts to a uniform—
white shirts, dark ties, and dark pants sometimes just slightly
rumpled; serious young men who speak quietly and move
quietly.

Some men spend their lives operating machines; others

shuffle papers in an office, or juggle figures. Without ever leaving the ground, these men spend their lives far up in the mists of airspace.

Controllers work in three shifts; 7 AM to 3 PM, 3 PM to 11 PM, and 11 PM to 7 AM. But adding the overtime makes it another matter, and a man may be exhausted before he heads out to the parking lot to drive home. Most controllers own their own homes and live in small towns near the airports or centers where they work, and nearly all have small children whom, they complain bitterly, they seldom see.

Disturbed about what most consider the excessive overtime they are often asked to work, and the fact that advanced electronic equipment has been very slow in arriving, controllers have formed a strong, aggressive union, the Professional Air Traffic Controllers Organization, known as PATCO. Chiefly PATCO is concerned about the quality of many new controllers now being granted certificates. They want the FAA to insist on higher standards and require at least two years of college and a pilot's license for such men. They want controllers to be rated by other controllers rather than by FAA executives. And finally they want pensions of fifty percent of final pay after twenty years of work, with no man working beyond the age of 45. This is not unreasonable when you consider that a controller has comparatively few jobs open to him after he stops working for the FAA.

The business of retirement is a very difficult one. When a controller is getting to be forty and isn't as sharp as he used to be, he can be moved to a position where there is lighter traffic, perhaps in a smaller city. Or he can go to ocean control, where there are no radarscopes to watch. But very often that will mean a cut in pay, something few men want to face, although some have accepted this rather than continue working in a tense situation. Today, and until many more controllers are trained, many of these older men will be kept in busy spots, although both the FAA and the men themselves would rather they were elsewhere. There simply are not enough controllers for our booming, expanding air traffic at present.

When they do leave their jobs as controllers, men do all sorts of things. Many get into selling life insurance or real estate, businesses they can start while they are still working as controllers. Since their shifts are changed frequently, they have a good deal of free time on certain days.

A few become supervisors or executives in the FAA. Some get advisory jobs with airlines, or jobs as pilots for executive planes. They can't get jobs as pilots with airlines, however, unless they start very early, for while airlines allow pilots to work until they are sixty, they almost never hire a man over thirty-two. One ex-controller has a job in Washington representing a manufacturer of aeronautical equipment. Some are flight instructors for private pilots. And at least one former controller is a Wall Street broker. Smart, knowledgeable men, they make out somehow.

Alphanumerics. Electronic system of reporting data about
    plane in flight in small blocks of illuminated letters
    and numbers on face of radarscope

Altimeter. Instrument showing a plane's altitude

ARINC. Short for Aeronautical Radio Inc.; a radio tele-
    phone network through which planes can be
    reached almost anywhere at sea or over the U.S.

Brainbag. Oversized briefcase in which pilot carries maps,
    bulletins, papers

Center. One of the 21 divisions of the airspace over the U.S.

Doppler System. Over-water navigation system using radar
    scanning of the ocean surface

Enroute Controller. A man working in an aircraft control
    Center; usually not concerned with takeoffs or
    landings

Eurocontrol. Organization controlling flights over several
    European countries

105
Special
Terms
Used
in
This
Book

Flight Progress Strip. Strip of paper about eight inches long on which controllers record data about a plane's flight

General Aviation. All privately owned planes

Handoff. A transfer of responsibility for a plane from one controller to another, as "I got a handoff . . ."

Holding Pattern. Section of airspace in which planes circle while waiting to land

Human Navigation. Determining a plane's position with a sextant, using the sun, moon or stars

Igloo. Cargo container shaped to slide inside a passenger plane after the seats are all removed

Inertial Navigation. System using small gyroscopes, like tops, to keep track of a plane's movements

Itinerant. Controller's term for a private plane

IFR. Instrument flight rules

Laddering planes down. In a holding pattern, bringing all the planes down 1,000 feet each, one after another, after the bottom plane has left the stack

LORAN. System of navigation over oceans, using beams sent out from towers

Missed approach. Failure of pilot to land on indicated runway

Navaids. Aerial navigation aids, such as maps and VOR (Visual Omni-Range) stations

Near miss. Situation in which two planes come dangerously close

QC plane. A quick-change passenger plane which can be converted into a cargo carrier after seats have been removed

Rate of closure. Speed with which two planes would crash if on collision course

Seat van. Special vehicle to hold seats removed from a plane

Sector. A subdivision of the airspace in a Center used in controlling aircraft

Separation. Space between planes in flight

Shrimp boats. Small clear-plastic markers which controllers place over a plane's blips on a radarscope. Data

106
*Special
Terms
Used
in
This
Book*

about each plane are written on marker with wax pencil.

Squawk code. Number given to a plane on a particular flight which identifies it for the alphanumerics display on the radarscope

Squawk ident. Identification of a plane's blips on a radarscope through the operation of a transponder in that plane

Terminal Controller. Man in an airport handling takeoffs and arrivals

Transponder. Device in a plane that broadcasts a special signal which changes the appearance of a plane's blips on the radarscope

VFR. Visual Flight Rules

VOR. Visual Omni-Range; VOR stations send out signals used in navigation all over the U.S.

Zulu Time. Controllers' term for Greenwich Mean Time (GMT). This uses the 24-hour clock. Twelve o'clock noon is written 12.00Z.